working with
# auras

# working with
# auras

## your complete guide to
## health and wellbeing

Jane Struthers

A GODSFIELD BOOK
www.godsfield.co.uk

For Margaret and Lesley, with much love

First published in Great Britain in 2006 by
Godsfield Press, a division of Octopus Publishing Group Ltd
2–4 Heron Quays, London, E14 4JP

Distributed in the United States and Canada by
Sterling Publishing Co., Inc.
387 Park Avenue South, New York, NY 10016-8810

ISBN-13: 978-1-84181-302-8
ISBN-10: 1-84181-302-8

A CIP catalogue record for this book is available from the British Library.

Printed and bound in China

2 4 6 8 10 9 7 5 3 1

# contents

# INTRODUCTION

Auras have fascinated me for as long as I can remember. As a child, I used to study the auras around the heads of the figures in religious paintings, and I still love to look at them. At that time, I did not realize that everyone has an aura; I thought they were confined to highly evolved souls, such as the great religious teachers and saints. Now I know that every object, animate or inanimate, has its own aura. This is the energetic envelope that surrounds everyone and everything.

I have always been sensitive to atmospheres and places, even to the point of sensing and seeing ghosts. But it was years before I realized I was tuning into the auras of places, and that these auras had retained the imprint of some of the people who knew them and the events that took place in them. Sometimes I would instinctively know something about someone, without having to be told. I was reading that person's aura, even though I was unaware of doing so.

As I started to read and learn more about auras, spirits and energy fields, I became intrigued by the idea of healing with my hands and started to practise on myself. It worked. I began to practise on other people as well, and that worked too. Once again, I was working with auras. I could not see them, but I could feel them.

I did not think that I would be able to see my own aura, or that of anyone else. I thought it was a special privilege reserved for other people. All that changed one spring day in 1999. My husband and I had spent the weekend with my cousin and her boyfriend at a healing centre. We had had a great time together, and were standing in bright sunshine in the car park,

chatting before driving back home. While we were talking, I glanced down at my watch to see what the time was.

I was transfixed. I could see my aura! It was a very clear, bright blue, and it extended for about a centimetre (half an inch) all round my fingers, wrist and arm. I blinked in amazement and it disappeared. But I knew it would come back. Having seen it once, and with such clarity, I knew I would be able to see it again. And I have. It is still bright blue, although when I fractured my right wrist and had to have two bones wired back in place the aura around that hand turned pale grey with murky brown streaks at the site of the breaks.

Perhaps you can already see your own aura and you would like know more about it, or maybe you are starting to learn about it and want to be able to see it for yourself. Whatever stage you have reached in learning about auras and working with them, I hope this book will help you to develop your aura-reading skills.

Jane Struthers

*We are all surrounded by our auras, even though we may not be able to see them.*

# the benefits of working with your aura

**The aura is a very important part of the human body. Most of us cannot see it without effort unless we are psychic or clairvoyant. However, even if you were not born with these gifts, you can still train yourself to see your aura, purely through practice and patience.**

There are many benefits to learning to work with your aura, as you will soon discover. You can scan your own aura to gain valuable information about your energy levels, the general state of your health, your mental clarity, your emotions and your moods.

## cleansing and strengthening your aura

When you begin to work with your aura, you will learn how to keep it clean. You can do this in several ways, all of which are described in this book, and you will soon notice the benefits of regularly cleansing your aura. You will feel better physically, your mind will be sharper and your emotions will be clearer. You might even notice that physical ailments start to clear up, apparently all by themselves.

When you learn to strengthen your aura, you will discover how to protect it against negative or unhelpful energies. You will learn how to ground yourself, so you are fully connected to the Earth and are able to absorb more of its life-giving energy. Instead of feeling drained by people who seem to draw all the energy out of you, you will learn how to protect yourself against their neediness. You will be stronger both physically and emotionally, instead of feeling as though you are being blown this way and that by the demands of others.

Strengthening your aura will also enable you to protect yourself from the electromagnetic pollution that surrounds us in the 21st century. You will gain an increased understanding of which foods are good for you and which are not, purely on the basis of how you feel when you touch or eat them. This information could improve your health.

## improved relationships

Your relationships will also benefit from working with your aura, because you will be more in touch with your true self. You will understand how we connect with each other on an energetic level, and how one person's aura can attract or repel another's. When you learn to cleanse your aura after a difficult experience with someone, you will have stopped yourself carrying around the residual emotions or passing them on to someone else. You will also feel much better.

## understanding colours

Working with your aura will lead to increased understanding of the importance of colour in your life. You will discover which colours are most prevalent in your aura, and what they mean. This will lead on to learning how to choose the colour you project to others, which will enhance your relationships. You will also realize why you like some colours more than others, and how you can choose which colours to wear for a particular purpose.

## feeling comfortable at home

This book will also teach you how to feel more comfortable when you are at home, by testing the aura of objects before you buy them and by cleansing the aura of any objects that are still harbouring the energy of previous owners or unpleasant experiences.

# WHAT IS AN AURA?

Everyone and everything has its own aura. This is the envelope of energy that surrounds each animate and inanimate object. You have an aura. Your partner has an aura. Your children, friends, pets and belongings all have auras. In this chapter you will discover exactly what an aura is and what it looks like. You will discover how your own aura is intimately connected with your body, and learn about some of the layers that are contained within your aura.

You may never have seen or felt your own aura, but do not let that deter you from establishing a strong, conscious connection with it. It exists. All you need to do is to believe in it and to work with it on a regular basis. You already have an intimate relationship with your aura, although you may not be aware of it.

Think of your aura as your personal energy shield. It protects you from harmful outside influences, although occasionally it could probably do with some help from you, and it keeps your physical body in a healthy condition. It is your aura that feeds your body, not the other way round. So the sooner you recognize and honour it, the better you will feel.

# the aura:
# your personal energy shield

**Your physical body is contained within your skin, but your energetic body, commonly referred to as your aura, extends far beyond this. Your aura is a three-dimensional envelope of energy that surrounds your body in all directions, consisting of several layers of increasingly fine energetic material. You may not be able to see it yet, but that does not mean it does not exist.**

A human being's aura is egg-shaped. It extends above the crown of the head and below the feet, in front of the stomach and behind the back, thereby enclosing and protecting the entire body. Some people have relatively small auras that do not radiate far from their physical bodies. Others have much larger auras, especially if they are spiritually evolved. It is claimed that the great religious teachers, such as Jesus, Mohammed and the Buddha, had the ability to extend their auras to a depth of several kilometres when they wanted to attract followers. Most people, however, have auras that extend roughly a metre (3 ft) above, in front and behind them, and slightly less below them.

## the aura's connection with the human body

Your aura is the energetic counterpart of your physical body. Your aura cannot exist without your body, and your body cannot exist without your aura. It contains the blueprint of all your organs, blood vessels, muscles, bones and everything else that you need to function as a healthy human being. When a healer performs an operation on a patient, he does not touch her physical body but instead works on her aura. He has no need to touch his patient because he knows that whatever changes he makes to her aura will be translated to her physical body.

You can try this for yourself. If you have an itch on a part of your body, try scratching the air just above your skin. After a few seconds your itch will disappear as if by magic. Congratulations – you have just made conscious contact with your aura. Next time, you can take this one step

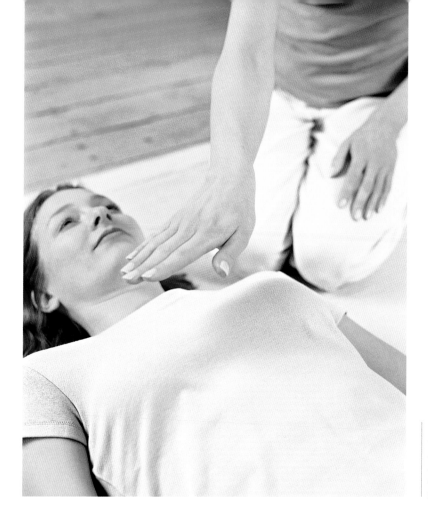

*Our auras are the energetic counterparts of our bodies. With the help of this book you will learn how to sense a person's aura with your hands, without touching her body.*

further by mentally scratching the itch. If you truly believe in what you are doing, the itch will go away.

## the size of auras

Generally speaking, a healthy human being has a strong, fairly large aura. Someone who is ill has a weak and small aura. However, you should not automatically assume that a small aura indicates illness. We all have the ability to contract our auras when necessary, even if we are not consciously aware of what we are doing, so there may be other reasons why someone has a small aura. For instance, they might have shrunk their aura in self-defence. We all instinctively contract our auras when we are confronted by someone we do not like, or when we find ourselves in a situation that makes us feel threatened. When you watch a frightening film and you shrink back in your seat, your aura will retreat with you.

# ancient and modern views

Humans have known about auras for thousands of years. Originally, they did not need scientific proof that auras existed because they could see them with their own eyes. They may have needed to see them in order to survive, perhaps so that they could diagnose illnesses in one another. As humans developed, however, they gained new skills and lost old ones that they no longer needed. One of these ancient skills was the ability to see auras, although very sensitive humans were still able to do so.

We know that our forebears believed in auras because they painted them. You only need to look at a religious painting to see the artist's interpretation of auras quite clearly. The auras were often depicted as haloes of light hovering over the crown of a person's head, or as a circle of golden light surrounding the entire head.

During the Victorian era there was a surge of interest in spirituality, prompting many people to write books about their experiences. Auras were often mentioned, and one notable example was a book called *The*

*Many medieval paintings show the auras of important religious figures. This painting depicts Jesus Christ and not only shows a golden aura around his head but a brightly coloured aura surrounding his body.*

*Boy Who Saw True*, about a young boy's experiences of seeing what he called 'lights' around people's heads. The author, who wrote the book anonymously, judged a person's character according to the colours of these lights. He was, of course, seeing people's auras. Since then, many mediums and sensitives have written books in which they describe their abilities to see auras, and how these have enabled them to help people.

## the modern understanding of auras

Some scientists dismiss the whole notion of auras as ridiculous, but others have been busy investigating them and trying to find out how they work and what they are made of. The research is fascinating because it validates what psychics and healers have known for centuries: that auras are composed of increasingly fine layers of energy that are continually vibrating and changing.

In Edwardian London, Dr Walter J. Kilner was one scientist who wanted to learn more about auras. He looked at the work his predecessors had carried out on auras and decided that, if such things really did exist and they changed according to the health of the patient, they would be a wonderful diagnostic tool for doctors. He invented what are called Kilner screens, through which he could view the aura, and announced he could see three layers of it.

In the mid-1930s in America, two scientists from Yale called Harold Saxton Burr and F.S.C. Northrop developed the theory that all living creatures are surrounded by an electrical field. They were able to prove this with a voltmeter.

Another scientist who has conducted extensive work on the aura is Dr Victor Inyushin, who works at Kazakh University in Russia. He believes the aura is composed of matter that he has called a 'bioplasmic' energy field containing ions, protons and electrons. It is very different from the four states of matter we have been familiar with until now: plasma, gases, liquids and solids.

As research continues, new discoveries will inevitably be made. Yet you do not need to keep up to date with scientific breakthroughs in order to work with your aura. All you need to do is to believe in it and to want to get to know it.

# photographing the aura

**If you are longing to discover what your aura looks like and do not want to wait until you have learned to see it for yourself, you can always have it photographed. This process uses a special camera, and you will often find stalls providing aura photography at mind, body and spirit fairs. On the internet, you can also find companies that photograph auras.**

However, before you start you should be aware that there are two main ways of photographing the aura: Kirlian photography and aura photography. It is often assumed that they are the same process, but they are not. Kirlian photography records the electromagnetic field that surrounds a person's body (although it can also be used on plants and animals), while aura photography gives an impression of what that field might look like.

*This is an example of Kirlian photography. Note the very long electromagnetic flares emanating from the person's head.*

## kirlian photography

In 1939, Professor Semyon Kirlian was visiting a hospital in Krasnodar in his native Russia when he witnessed a peculiar phenomenon. A patient was being treated with a new, high-frequency generator. When glass electrodes were placed close to the patient's skin, there was a tiny flash of light. This meant something was charging the electrodes, but what? Kirlian was determined to find out, so he began to experiment on himself. He sandwiched his hand between two metal plates and took a photograph of what happened when he switched on an electric current. He had captured the outline of his hand surrounded by a corona of light. He soon realized the significance of this: he had photographed his own aura.

Kirlian photography, as the process has become known, is now a celebrated way of capturing a person's aura on camera. It releases electrons that reveal the electromagnetic field surrounding that person. The process is especially successful when used to photograph hands and feet; they contain so many nerve endings that they emit strong electromagnetic fields, which show up well on camera.

Practitioners of Kirlian photography analyse the results to draw conclusions about a person's emotional, mental and physical states. Very often one hand produces a stronger aura than the other. This can be very revealing as the right hand is believed to relate to a person's thought processes and the left hand to their emotional responses, regardless of whether that person is left- or right-handed.

The results of Kirlian photography depend on the type of film used and also, of course, on the emotions, mental state and physical condition of the person whose photograph is being taken. Nevertheless, Kirlian photographs can reveal a fascinating kaleidoscope of colours surrounding a person, and therefore provide a wealth of information about their aura.

*This example of aura photography shows the entire person and not just an outline. The signals emanating from the man's aura have been translated into colours by the camera.*

## aura photography

This uses an entirely different process from Kirlian photography. Aura photography uses sensors that are placed on the subject's skin. These sensors take readings that are then fed into an electronic processor which translates the information into the form of signals. These signals are sent to a special camera, which interprets them as colours and produces a coloured image surrounding the person. Sometimes the camera operator will intuitively tune into the person's aura and adjust the colours and shapes produced by the camera accordingly. Therefore the resulting image is not a photograph of the aura but the operator's impression of what that might look like.

# what an aura looks like

**When you first train yourself to see your aura, you will probably only see a small part of it. This is the section nearest to your physical body, and it is called the etheric body. However, your aura extends a long way past this, and you will gradually learn to see at least part of it.**

## colour and density

There is no set colour for auras. One person may have a predominantly blue aura, while another person's may be mostly green or yellow. Each colour has its own significance, as you will learn later in this book. Whichever colour you can see around a person or around yourself, it looks like a haze of shimmering light. With practice, you will notice that this light-filled aura appears to be composed of many individual lights that are in perpetual motion. If you practise deep breathing while watching your aura, you will see it expand.

Our auras are densest nearest to our bodies, and become increasingly fine as they extend outwards. They look like bands of solid colour, although they are not as dense as physical objects. In fact, looking at an aura is rather like gazing at a rainbow in the sky. You know it is not solid, although it looks as if it is.

## auras and our ages

Our auras change to reflect our circumstances, moods and state of health. They also reflect our development from baby to child, from child to adolescent, and from adolescent to adult.

You could try looking at the aura of a young baby asleep in his cot, provided that he is lying on a

*As children grow, their auras go through a similar process of maturation. This young boy's aura is just starting to develop.*

light-coloured, plain sheet. Although it might be tempting to study the baby while he is being cradled in your arms, your own aura will quickly merge with his and you will therefore not get an accurate impression of his aura. When you do see it, you will notice that it is pale grey and fuzzy. This is because it has yet to develop fully. At this stage in the baby's development, his aura is still closely connected to that of his mother.

A child's aura has more definition than a baby's, and becomes more colourful as she grows older. However, children rarely stay still for long so you may not have much opportunity to study a child's aura before she has jumped up and run off to do something else. You may even have to study her while she is asleep.

When an adolescent is going through puberty, his aura really starts to develop. As you might imagine, sometimes his aura will look calm and controlled and at other times, when his hormones and emotions are raging, it will be in a state of chaos.

*This woman has a good, strong aura. Its green colour reveals that she is a loving and peaceful person.*

An adult's aura is much more settled. It may even have become stagnant and blocked because the person has become too set in his ways.

## auras in sickness and in health

Someone who is healthy has a strong, vibrant aura. It is a good, clear colour, and feels elastic and resilient when you touch it. However, someone who is unwell has a much weaker aura. It is pale in colour and may have muddy, dark blotches trapped within it. If you touch it, it will feel flabby and flaccid, as though it has lost its energy.

# the layers of the aura

**When you first teach yourself to view auras, you will probably only see a small area of coloured light, less than 2.5 cm (1 in) deep, next to your body. You could be forgiven for thinking that this is the full extent of your aura, but actually it is only the beginning of it. It is relatively easy to see because it is composed of dense energy and it has strong connections with your physical body.**

*This diagram shows how the layers of a healthy aura extend outwards in an egg shape and tuck under the feet. Each layer of the aura penetrates the layers beneath it.*

In fact, your aura consists of several layers. There is some debate among people who study auras, but it is generally agreed that a human aura has seven layers. This suggests that each layer is separate and quite distinct from its neighbours, but that is misleading. It would be more accurate to say that each layer of the aura penetrates the layers that lie beneath it, and they all envelop the physical body. Each successive layer vibrates at a higher frequency than the one below it, and is composed of finer energy. These layers of the aura become increasingly fine as they radiate outwards, so the outermost layers can usually only be seen by people when they are in a meditative state and using their intuition.

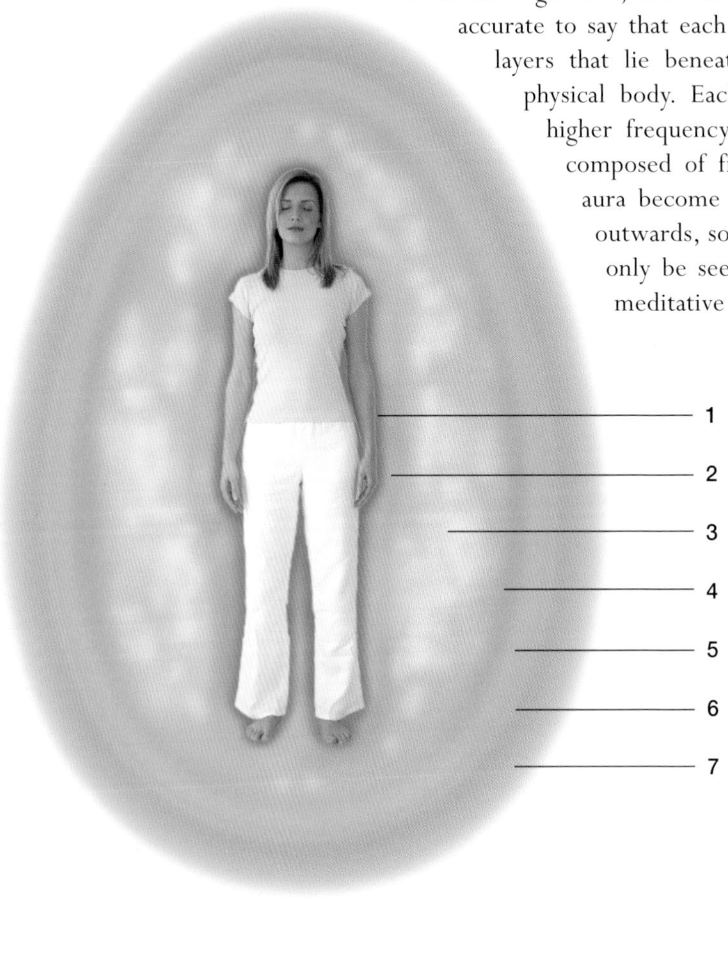

1

2

3

4

5

6

7

## the seven layers

You will find different names for these layers in different books, especially for the four outermost layers. The exact terminology does not really matter; what is important is to understand how each layer functions and how it affects us.

1 **The etheric body** is nearest to the human body, and is therefore the densest. It is the one you see when you first start to practise viewing auras, and varies in colour from pale grey to bright blue. The condition of the etheric body closely reflects that of the physical body.

2 **The emotional body** is the next layer and, as its name suggests, it relates to the emotions. The nature of a person's emotions appear as clouds of coloured energy within the aura. These clouds changes colour as the person's emotions change, so they describe passing moods.

3 **The mental body** is the third layer. As you would expect from its name, it is connected with a person's thought processes. It is predominantly yellow, but you will also see thought forms within it. The stronger and more ingrained these are, the greater is their definition within the mental body. The colour of these thought forms shows the nature of the emotions that are connected to them.

4 **The astral layer** is the fourth layer of the aura and is connected to love and relationships. It is the dividing line between the three inner layers, which relate to the physical world, and the three outer layers, which relate to the spiritual world.

5 **The etheric template** is a blueprint of the physical body and the etheric layer. It relates to the physical body on a spiritual level, so healing is very effective when it is performed on this template.

6 **The celestial body** is the sixth layer of the aura. It relates to the emotions on a spiritual level, and is the layer at which we experience unconditional love.

7 **The ketheric template** is the seventh layer of the aura. It relates to the mental processes on a spiritual level, and is where we become one with the universe.

# LEARNING TO SENSE
# AND SEE YOUR AURA

Many young children are able to see the auras of people, animals, plants and other objects. They retain this perfectly natural ability until the adult world starts to intrude, possibly with grown-ups telling them that they are imagining things when they describe the coloured lights they can see around someone's head. Gradually, children block out their ability to see auras because it gets them into too much trouble, or they are wary of appearing different or weird.

Perhaps you were able to see auras when you were a child; in this case, you must re-educate your eyes into seeing them again. Keep practising and do not give up trying, even if your ability to see auras fluctuates at first. It is mostly a matter of believing in what you are doing, and of knowing that you will eventually succeed in seeing and sensing your own aura. Do not be defeatist or negative about this, because then you will sabotage your ability to see your aura. You should also be patient and persistent, as well as prepared to experiment. Practise the exercises for seeing your aura in different lighting conditions and different rooms, until you find the combination that works for you.

*When you first start to practise seeing auras it is very important for you to be in a relaxed and balanced state before you begin.*

# tuning in to auras

It is much easier to see an aura, whether it belongs to you or someone else, than you might imagine. For most people, it only takes a couple of minutes for them to begin to detect an aura. Once they have made this initial jump from seeing nothing to seeing something, they are on the path to seeing auras in more detail. This is true for you, too.

## how to see auras

There are two ways in which we are able to see the aura of another human being, another living creature (such as a pet) and even an apparently inanimate object. The first is by simply observing it with your eyes, and the second is by observing it with your mind's eye. Some people get better results from using their eyes, and some find it much easier to use their inner vision.

It does not matter which method you use. There is no right or wrong way to view an aura, and no psychic pecking order that declares one method is superior or more enlightened than the other. It is simply a question of how your mind and eyes work. If you have poor or impaired vision, you might struggle to see someone's aura simply by observing it with your physical eyes because they are unable to give you the results you want. However, you should not despair because you will find that, once you start training it and trusting the images it produces, your mind's eye will reveal what you are looking for. The following pages describe how to view auras with your eyes, but here is how to view them with your mind's eye.

## how to see with your mind's eye

You already do this, often without even being aware of it, when you think of anything that triggers your imagination. For instance, whenever you remember an event you are seeing it with your mind's eye. You do not have to make any special effort; it happens quite spontaneously and can be such a vivid experience that you no longer see your surroundings because mentally you have been transported somewhere else.

You will have the same experience when you start viewing auras with your mind's eye. All you need to do is to look closely at the object whose aura you want to study, fix its image in your mind, and then look away. Either close your eyes or keep them open, and conjure up the image of the object. You might see it in plenty of detail or simply as a silhouette, according to the way your mind works. Can you see an aura around it? Trust the image that comes to you and resist any temptation to tinker with it if it does not match what you were expecting to see. Jot down what you have seen, either in words or pictures, so you can compare the image with what you see next time you perform this exercise. Above all, keep practising until it is second nature to use your mind's eye to view auras, and believe in what you are doing.

# feeling is believing

**When you first start to practise seeing and feeling auras, it can take time to gradually build up your expertise. Some people have no problems in seeing, feeling and sensing auras almost immediately, while others find it takes a while before they get any tangible results.**

No matter how long it takes you to see and feel auras, you will need someone to practise on, and the best person to choose is yourself. You can then go at your own pace, whereas if you work with someone else they might get restless or bored, and neither mood will be conducive to tuning into their aura.

## discovering what your aura feels like

Before you move on to the exciting business of actually looking at your aura, you are going to practise feeling it. This will help you to tune into your aura and will also increase your self-confidence, so you will have greater success when you start to view your aura. The most effective way to begin, because it brings such quick results, is to play with the aura surrounding your hands. Our hands are very sensitive areas of our bodies, packed with nerve endings that enable us to touch and feel objects with tremendous sensitivity. As you will discover later in this book, our hands also contain energy centres known as minor chakras, which are easily activated and rewarding.

The exercise given here will help you to tune into the aura around your hands and produce a ball of energy. Keep practising this exercise so you become more experienced at feeling this energy ball. As you do so, you will notice that your hands become increasingly sensitive.

## playing with the energy ball

1 Sit quietly by yourself and place both feet flat on the floor. Take several deep breaths to calm and balance yourself. Tell yourself that you are going to sense the aura around your hands, and believe that you will be able to do this.

2 Bring your hands close together until the palms are about 5 cm (2 in) away from each other. Spend a couple of minutes feeling the heat building up between your palms. Pay attention to any other sensations that you might experience, such as tingling in the palms of your hands.

3 Gently move the palms of your hands about 10 cm (4 in) apart and then bring them close together again. Do not let your hands touch each other. Now increase the speed at which you move your palms, as if you were clapping your hands but without letting them touch each other.

4 As you move your hands back and forth, the space between them will start to feel different. It usually feels bouncy and elastic, and as you separate your hands it will feel as though it is stretching. As you bring your hands together, you will feel a springy pressure between them and may get the sensation that the energy is being compressed or is squeezing out around the edges of your hands. You are now feeling the aura around your hands.

# sensing your aura using bodywork

**At this stage, it is important to practise feeling your aura so that the entire process becomes increasingly familiar to you. As you continue to work, you will become more confident and you will be able to tune into your aura more quickly each time. Look on the whole experience as an enjoyable exercise by playing with the aura around your entire body and not just your hands. Keep working at it.**

## energy follows thought

This is a very important rule to remember, especially on those days when you feel you are not making much progress or you are still trying to sense the energy ball between your hands (see page 27). When you send out a thought, it is followed by energy. So, if you repeatedly send out the thought that you want to feel the aura around your body, energy will follow that thought and enable you to carry out your wish. Know that your aura surrounds your body, and that you will eventually be able to feel it. Believe in what you are doing.

## sensing the depth and strength of your aura

After you have become familiar with the exercise shown here, you can start to sense the depth and strength of your aura. Begin to experiment with it. Is it stronger at a particular time of day, such as the morning or evening? Is it stronger when you are hungry or after you have eaten? How strong is it when you do not feel very well? Does sunshine make a difference to it?

# feeling the aura around your body

1 Set aside some time when you will not be disturbed and you can relax. If possible, switch on your telephone answering machine so you do not have to take any calls. Take off any jewellery that will make a noise and distract you, such as metal bangles or bracelets. Activate the energy centres in your hands by creating an energy ball (see page 27).

2 Hold your right hand, palm downwards, about 5 cm (2 in) above your left forearm. Do not touch your arm because then you will not be able to feel your aura. Move your right hand slowly up and down above your left arm, taking note of any sensations you experience.

3 You will soon start to feel a cushion of energy between your right hand and your left arm. This is your aura. Move your hand further up your left arm and repeat the exercise.

4 Now switch arms, holding your left palm above your right forearm. Does it feel any different? Is one hand more sensitive than the other? Continue the exercise on other parts of your body, such as your legs and feet. Keep practising the exercise so you become better acquainted with your aura and more accomplished at sensing it.

# preparing to see your aura

**After experimenting with the feel of your aura, you are now ready to move on to the next stage, which is to look at your aura. This is a very exciting process and you will be thrilled when you first catch a glimpse of your own aura. However, you stand the greatest chance of being successful at seeing your aura if you take this process gently and choose the right time to practise. You are less likely to see something if you are in a hurry, or are sitting in a room with other people who keep staring at you or who ask you what on earth you are doing.**

Ideally, you should be by yourself, feeling relaxed and with no urgent appointments or tasks to drag you away from what you are doing. Before you begin to look at your aura, you must put your body and mind into a state of relaxation by practising the balancing exercise given opposite.

## believing in what you are doing

You will never see an aura if you are busy telling yourself that such things do not exist or that you are not psychic or special enough. So it is very important for you to believe wholeheartedly in what you are doing and to keep assuring yourself that you are able to see auras.

Although later on, when you are more practised at viewing auras, you will probably enjoy discussing them with other people, at this stage it might be better to avoid talking about them, in case you are discouraged by what people say to you. Even if you hear a flippant or dismissive comment and think you have forgotten it, it could come back to haunt you when you start looking at your own aura and might make you doubt what you are doing. You must also banish any negative self-talk from your mind, especially if your initial attempts to see your aura are not as successful as you had hoped.

## balancing and relaxing the body and mind

1 Choose a time when you can be quietly by yourself, with no interruptions. Sit in a comfortable chair, with both feet on the floor. Let your hands lie loosely in your lap and close your eyes.

2 Slowly breathe in and out through your nose several times. With each in-breath, imagine that you are inhaling a sense of relaxation, and with each out-breath imagine that you are exhaling any stress or tension that you may be feeling.

3 Continue to breathe slowly and rhythmically and, as you do so, relax your feet. Feel all the tension drain out of them. Now relax your ankles, followed by your shins and calves, then your knees, then your thighs, and continue in this way until you have reached the top of your head.

4 At first it will take you several minutes to perform this exercise, but with practice it will become much quicker for you to achieve this state of mental balance and physical relaxation. You will eventually be able to achieve it in a matter of seconds.

# believing is seeing

**You are now ready to practise seeing your own aura. If you have never seen it before, you must gradually acclimatize your eyes so they can see what has been invisible to you until now. It is not as though you will be magically creating something that has not existed until this moment. Instead, you will be training your eyes to see something that already exists but which, for some reason, you have not noticed. Believe that you will see your aura, even if it takes a while for you to do so.**

## what you can expect to see

The best way to start is to look at the aura around your own hands. Choose a relatively dim room in which to do this because bright sunshine or artificial light will be stronger than your aura and may make it hard for you to see. At first, this aura will appear as a white or pearly grey translucence that extends about a centimetre (half an inch) around your hands. As you continue to look at it, it will suddenly disappear. This is quite normal, and generally means that you have been looking at it directly. You will have much greater success at studying your own aura if you look beyond or to one side of it, in exactly the same way that you might look at a particular star in the night sky.

At first it will take a couple of minutes for the aura around your hands to become visible. However, this process will speed up as you continue to practise. You will also begin to see the colour of the aura around your hands. This will be an exciting and encouraging development, but do not be dismayed if it does not happen as quickly as you would like. It simply means that your eyes are taking a long time to develop their new vision or that you are unconsciously preventing yourself seeing the colours, perhaps because you keep telling yourself that you are not special enough.

## learning to see the aura around your hands

1  Sit in a dimly lit room, facing a pale-coloured wall. Put yourself into a relaxed and balanced state (see page 31). Hold your right hand in front of you with your fingers splayed apart.

2  Look just above or to one side of the tips of your fingers, so you are not looking directly at them. Now allow your eyes to relax. As they continue to relax, you will start to see a grey or white image appearing around each finger. This is your aura.

3  As you continue to gaze into the space beside or above your fingers, the grey or white image will suddenly take on a colour, such as blue or green. Do not move your eyes to look directly at it, because that will make it disappear. Observe it until it vanishes of its own accord or your eyes get tired.

4  Rest for a couple of minutes, then repeat the exercise with your left hand. At first you may find it easier to see the aura of one hand than of the other, so keep practising until you can see them both clearly.

# looking further

**When you have mastered the ability to see the aura around your hands, you are more than halfway towards viewing the aura of anything else, whether it is an animate or inanimate object. The next step is to look at the aura around your own head, and around the heads of other people.**

The easiest way to observe the aura around your own head is to look at your reflection in a mirror. Choose a mirror in a room with plain, light walls so you will not be distracted by strong patterns or colours.

If you want to observe the aura around someone else's head, you must remember a few basic rules. The most important rule is to always ask her permission first, because you are observing a very personal and private part of this person. Looking at a person's aura is like raking through her personal belongings, especially when you become skilled enough to see her aura in a lot of detail. You should also explain what you are going to do before you start, so the person knows what to expect. Try to put her at ease, and to relax yourself, to avoid an embarrassing atmosphere that will undoubtedly inhibit your aura-reading abilities.

*You must always ask permission before looking at another person's aura because it is a very private part of that person.*

Continue to practise these exercises so that you become more adept and it takes less time for the aura around your own head, and that of other people, to become visible. As you do this, start to notice whether your aura is stronger at some times of the day than others, and whether it is easier to see in the morning or evening. For instance, you may find that your faculties are much sharper first thing in the morning, or that your aura is much easier to see last thing at night when you feel sleepy and relaxed.

## looking at the aura around your own head

1 Choose a time when you will be undisturbed and stand in front of a mirror that is lit by natural light. Perform the relaxation exercise (see page 31).

2 Look in the mirror at the area above the crown of your head. Look beyond it rather than directly at it. Allow your eyes to relax.

3 You will start to see a fuzz of light around your head. This is your aura. Continue to look beyond it and see whether it develops any colours.

## looking at the aura around someone else's head

1 Ask someone for permission to look at the aura around her head. Ask her to stand or sit in front of a plain, light-coloured wall. Perform the relaxation exercise (see page 31).

2 Look at the area above and beyond the crown of her head, and allow your eyes to relax.

3 You will start to see a fuzz of light around her head, which is her aura. Continue to look beyond it and wait to see if it develops any colours. Remember to not look directly at it. When you have finished, thank the person for letting you look at her aura.

# THE AURA-CHAKRA CONNECTION

You may already be familiar with the concept of chakras in the human body. These are the seven major energy centres that run vertically through the body, from the top of the head to the base of the trunk. They are the crown chakra, the brow chakra, the throat chakra, the heart chakra, the solar plexus chakra, the sacral chakra, and the base (or root) chakra. In addition, there are 21 minor chakras, including those that are located in the palms of the hands and the soles of the feet. Together, the major and minor chakras are an intricate energy system that keeps the human body in a state of optimum health.

The word 'chakra' comes from the Sanskrit, meaning 'wheel'. That is because chakras are traditionally thought of as wheels of energy, and when they are operating at their best they continually spin round. When they are blocked or not functioning properly, the rate at which they spin slows down and they become sluggish.

Each chakra is intimately connected with the aura that surrounds it, and the state of the chakra therefore has a profound impact on a person's aura. When a chakra is not working efficiently, the neighbouring sections of the aura will be adversely affected and will eventually manifest in the body as emotional or physical ailments. It is therefore very important to keep the chakras in good working order.

# the major chakras

**There are seven major chakras in the human body, located at intervals from the crown of the head to beneath the genitals. In addition, there are minor chakras that we will discuss later in this section (see pages 44–47).**

## where are the chakras?

To understand where the chakras are, and to see them in your imagination, you must picture them running in a straight vertical line through the centre of the human body. The illustrations on the opposite page and on page 41 will help you to do this. However, the chakras are energetic centres and are not physical, so you would not find them if you could see inside a human body.

Each chakra is usually shown as being midway between the front and back of the physical body, but in fact the chakras radiate out much further than this and extend through all the layers of the aura.

## what are the chakras?

Each chakra is a high point of energy in the aura. Fine networks of energy run throughout the aura in a series of lines, and each line of energy is called a 'nadi', which is another Sanskrit word. The places where a large number of these nadis intersect are the chakras. The major chakras are formed at the points in the aura where the greatest number of nadis intersect, while the minor chakras are formed where a smaller number of nadis meet.

The major chakras are therefore highly charged areas within the aura, and they influence a specific part of the human body. The heart chakra, for example, is situated in the centre of the chest and influences the physical wellbeing of the heart and lungs. Yet each chakra also has a specific effect on the emotions. For example, the crown chakra affects the ability to connect with the higher self, while the base chakra is concerned with emotional and physical grounding.

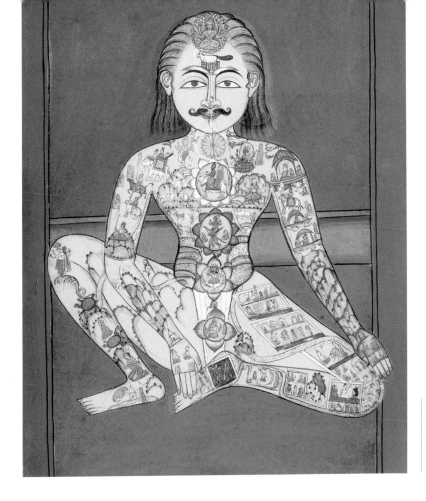

*The chakra system is believed to come from Eastern yogic traditions and is centuries old. The seven main chakras are painted down the centre of the man's body in this illustration.*

## how chakras affect the aura and the body

Chakras are extremely important centres of energy within the aura, so the way they function will affect the aura and, eventually, the human body. If a chakra is blocked with stagnant energy or is leaking energy for some reason, it will not function properly and, over time, the area of the body that it influences will become impaired. Clear, unhampered chakras lead to better health, greater vitality and improved mental abilities because the body is working at its best.

Rather than thinking of the physical body affecting the state of the chakras, you need to reverse the idea and realize it is the chakras that eventually affect the body. If they are not dealt with, persistent problems, blockages and imbalances in the chakras will finally manifest as physical ailments. These can be anything from impaired hearing, when the brow chakra is not functioning properly, to persistent digestive complaints when the base chakra is under pressure.

## the seven chakras

The chakras are traditionally numbered from one to seven, working from the base chakra up to the crown. Each of them has a specific function. You will find more information about them on pages 42–43.

1 **The base chakra** lies in the perineum, which is the space between the genitals and the anus. If this chakra is not functioning properly, energy will not be able to move through it and climb upwards to feed the other chakras. The person will feel out of touch with her surroundings and may not be fully present in her body. The base chakra affects our sense of being grounded in the here and now, and of being connected to the planet. It vibrates at the lowest rate of all the chakras because it is so strongly connected to the physical body.

2 **The sacral chakra** sits the width of two fingers below the navel. If this chakra is not functioning properly, the person will feel a lack of emotional security that can adversely affect her relationships. Her sense of physical security can also be impaired, which might lead to panic attacks or fears of venturing into the outside world. The sacral chakra influences our sexual organs so affects our creativity on every level, from conceiving a child and giving birth physically, to giving birth to creative and artistic projects.

3 **The solar plexus chakra** is located below the sternum. It governs the emotions, which is why our stomachs are strongly affected by our feelings. It also rules our self-esteem and sense of individuality, and therefore the way we relate to other people. A sluggish or blocked solar plexus chakra can lead to difficult relationships in which the person feels dominated by others, without the ability or right to exercise and express her own personality and opinions.

4 **The heart chakra** is in the centre of the chest. As its name implies, it rules the heart and describes our ability to show heartfelt compassion and love to others. It has powerful spiritual qualities as it rules our relationship with the Divine as well as with our fellow human beings. When this chakra cannot open properly, the person withholds her feelings and is stingy with her affection. When it is permanently open, as in the case of someone who has a genuine need to help others, it can lead to physical and emotional exhaustion.

5 **The throat chakra** is in the base of the throat, and it rules our ability to communicate with others and to find our own voice through self-expression. Difficulties with this chakra can lead to throat problems, such as chronic hoarseness, which place physical restrictions on the way we communicate with others.

6 **The brow chakra** is located on the bridge of the nose between the eyebrows. This is the site of the 'third eye', which is believed to give us insight and inspiration. Therefore this chakra gives us the power to be imaginative and to use our intellect. Using these abilities well gives us a sense of fulfilment; squandering or ignoring them leads to dissatisfaction. Problems with this chakra can lead to a stale and stagnant mind, as well as physical difficulties such as blocked sinuses.

7 **The crown chakra** is on the top of the head, near the crown. This is a very sensitive chakra and many people feel uncomfortable when others get too close to it. It rules our connection with our higher selves, as well as our spiritual hopes and development. When we connect with spirit or God, we do so through this chakra. Problems with this chakra can lead to depression and a debilitating sense of dissatisfaction.

*Although the chakras appear to sit on top of this woman's body, in reality they permeate all the layers of her aura.*

7

6

5

4

3

2

1

# the major chakras at a glance

| | CHAKRA | POSITION IN BODY | GLAND |
|---|---|---|---|
| | Crown | Top of the head | Pituitary |
| | Brow | Between the eyes | Pineal |
| | Throat | Neck | Thyroid and parathyroid |
| | Heart | Centre of chest | Thymus |
| | Solar plexus | Below the sternum | Pancreas |
| | Sacral | Two fingers below the navel | Gonads |
| | Base | Perineum | Adrenals |

| PARTS OF BODY | EMOTIONAL CONNECTION | COLOUR |
|---|---|---|
| Upper brain; right eye | Connection with higher self | Violet and white |
| Lower brain; left eye; ear, nose and throat; nervous system | Idealism and intuition | Indigo |
| Larynx | Communication and self-expression | Blue |
| Heart; lungs; immune system; vagus nerve | Compassion | Spring green and rose pink |
| Stomach; liver; gall bladder | Physical emotions | Yellow |
| Reproductive system; urinary tract; lower back | Creativity and imagination | Orange |
| Base of spine; rectum and bowel; bone marrow; kidneys | Emotional and physical balance | Red |

# the minor chakras

**Have you ever felt that someone was watching you, even though you had your back to him? That is because the minor chakras in the back of your head and the back of your shoulders were being activated by the person's gaze. When we speak of someone having 'eyes in the back of his head', we are actually referring to the minor chakras that are found there and which are busily registering what is going on.**

We may refer to these chakras as being 'minor', but that does not diminish their significance in any way. They are simply points in the aura where fewer nadis or lines intersect than at the major chakras, but they are still important energy centres that we use every day, often without consciously realizing it.

## the positions of the minor chakras

As you can see from the map, most of the minor chakras are situated in the upper body. There is one behind each eye; one on each cheek; one at the meeting point of the collarbones; one above each breast; one near the thymus gland; one near the stomach; two near the spleen; one near the liver; one near the solar plexus; one near each gonad; one in the palm of each hand; one behind each knee; and one on the sole of each foot.

## the hand chakras

The chakras in the palm of each hand are especially important because they are used by healers, masseurs and anyone else who heals others with their hands. They have a direct connection with the heart chakra, so compassion and love are channelled from a person's heart chakra down their arms and out through the chakras in their hands.

There are times when you need to close your hand chakras. For instance, if you habitually clean up after other people, or you are the first person everyone comes to when they are in trouble, your hand chakras may be permanently open. This means energy from your heart chakra is draining out through your hands, leading to emotional exhaustion and physical ailments. It is easy to close the chakras when you need to. Simply make a fist with each hand for a few seconds.

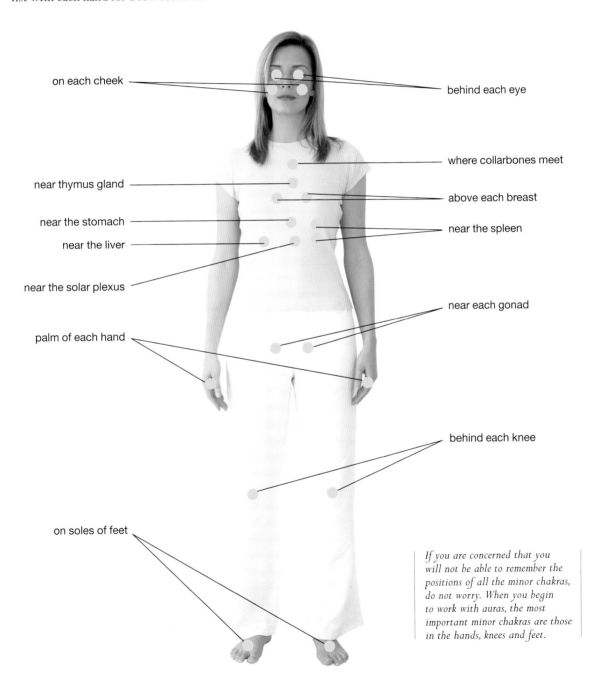

on each cheek

behind each eye

where collarbones meet

near thymus gland

above each breast

near the stomach

near the liver

near the spleen

near the solar plexus

near each gonad

palm of each hand

behind each knee

on soles of feet

*If you are concerned that you will not be able to remember the positions of all the minor chakras, do not worry. When you begin to work with auras, the most important minor chakras are those in the hands, knees and feet.*

*If your foot chakras are not activated you are not grounded, and if you are not grounded you are not absorbing enough energy from the earth beneath your feet. In time, this can lead to fatigue and possibly even illness, so it must be corrected.*

## the foot chakras

It is your foot chakras that enable you to ground yourself and to connect with the earth beneath you. They are therefore very important chakras and you should practise opening them, to ensure that they are operating efficiently. One way to do this is to take plenty of exercise, especially if that involves walking outdoors. Dancing is another excellent way of activating your feet chakras, and it will help to ground you at the same time. You can also practise the grounding exercise (see page 95) in order to ensure that you are fully connected to the earth. The soles of your feet will start to tingle and feel warm, which means your foot chakras have been activated.

If you often feel rather dizzy or disconnected from the world around you, it will help to wear red socks. Red is the colour connected to the base chakra (see page 40), and it will therefore help to keep you centred in your body. Red socks are also very helpful if you have poor circulation and your feet often feel cold.

## activating the chakras in your hands

If you want to do a lot of work with auras, or you would like to extend that to becoming a healer, you need to activate the chakras in the palms of your hands to make them more sensitive. The energy ball exercise (see page 27) is one way to do this, but here are two other options for you.

1 Hold your hands loosely by your sides, with your palms facing inwards. Now bring your palms together. Rub them together as rapidly as you can manage for about one minute. Your palms should be feeling tingly and hot. This warm tingle will continue when you separate your palms, telling you that you have activated your hand chakras. Try the energy ball exercise now, and see if it feels different from when you do not rub your palms together first.

2 Hold your hands loosely in front of you, then shake them back and forth for a few seconds. Can you feel a tingling or pulling in the centre of your palms? It may help to imagine the chakras opening.

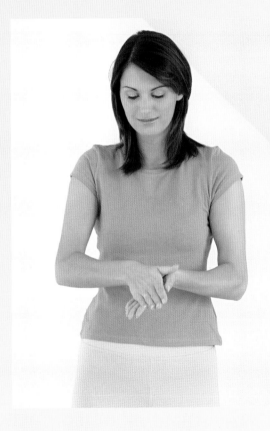

# scanning the chakras

**If you want to test your own chakras to make sure they are working efficiently, you can scan them. You can do this with a pendulum, with the palms of your hands if they are very sensitive, or by mentally looking at each chakra in turn. As with any form of exercise, the more you practise the more proficient you will become, so do not be disheartened if it takes you several attempts to locate the chakras or to get a reading from them.**

*When choosing a pendulum, you must look for one that feels right for you. It must also be able to swing easily on its chain or ribbon. In addition to pendulums made from crystals, they are also available in metal and wood.*

## locating the chakras within the aura

This is a lot easier than you may think. The person being scanned, whether it is you or someone else, should either be lying down or sitting in a chair. Simply hold the pendulum or the palm of your hand about 5 cm (2 in) above the relevant area on the front of the body, using the diagram of the major chakras (see pages 42–43). There is no need to touch the person's body.

## what the chakras feel like in the aura

If you are scanning someone with your hands, pay attention to what each chakra feels like: for instance, it might be hot or cold, heavy or light, sticky, fractured, lopsided, large or small. This will tell you whether the chakra is working well or if it needs help, perhaps because it is blocked or is leaking energy. With time, you may even be able to feel whether the chakra is spinning properly, and in which direction.

# dowsing the chakras

**1** If you already use a pendulum for dowsing, you will know which is its 'yes' and which is its 'no' response. If you are using a pendulum for the first time, you will have to train it to give you the correct response. Hold it over a glass of water and ask it if it is being held over a toy car. It should give you a particular response, such as an elliptical swing, to indicate 'no'. Now ask it if it is being held over a glass of water. It should give you a different sort of swing, such as a clockwise circle, to indicate 'yes'. Keep practising, using different objects, to train your pendulum to give you the correct answer each time.

**2** Now hold the pendulum over the base chakra. Either ask out loud if the chakra is functioning normally or do it silently. Notice the answer you get. Then progress to the sacral chakra and repeat the exercise. Continue in this way until you reach the crown chakra. If you are dowsing your own chakras, you will have to look in a mirror to see the responses you get when you reach your head. Remember that you will be seeing a mirror image of them, so you will have to reverse them.

**3** You will soon notice that a pendulum develops strange or irregular swings when a chakra is not working properly. The swings may vary from chakra to chakra. Use your intuition to understand what each swing might mean.

*An excellent way to establish a strong energy flow through your feet is to walk barefoot or to lie down on grass for at least ten minutes at a time.*

# increasing the energy flow

**There is a continual exchange of energy between our auras and the universe, although we may not be aware of it. In some of us, this exchange of energy works perfectly. We take in the energy we need and we send out energy in return. But the balance is out of kilter for some people, whether they suck in massive amounts of energy that they do not replace or they send out more energy than they allow themselves to receive.**

## how energy flows through the chakras

Just as trees are nourished through their roots, human beings receive energy through our chakras. We absorb the energy of the planet through the minor chakras in the soles of our feet and also through the crown chakra in the top of our head. We release energy through each of our chakras, but especially the heart and hand chakras. Incidentally, people who are amputees are still able to be part of this natural energy flow because, even if a limb is absent, its energetic equivalent still exists in the aura.

## how to establish a strong energy flow

If you often feel tired and sluggish, or you have a chronic illness, it is highly likely that energy is not flowing through your aura properly. Maybe there is a leak in a chakra so you lose the energy as fast as you absorb it, or perhaps you are not fully grounded and cannot take in enough energy through your feet. The exercise opposite will help.

## soaking up nature's energy

1 Ideally, you should perform this exercise in the open air on a warm day. You can use your own garden, a grassy park or a favourite stretch of countryside. Choose a patch of grass that looks inviting and comfortable, and lie down on it, flat on your back. Lie on a rug if the grass is damp. If you cannot lie down outside, simply imagine that you are doing so, and follow the rest of the exercise in your imagination. It will still be effective.

2 Close your eyes and allow your limbs to settle in a comfortable position. Breathe slowly and deeply, and as you do so feel all the tension melt out of your body into the ground beneath you. It might help to picture this happening. Feel the warmth of the sun on your body and the reassuring solidity of the ground beneath you. Listen to the sounds of nature around you and smell the air. Completely immerse yourself in your surroundings.

3 Now take a deep breath. As you do so, imagine that you are inhaling energy from your surroundings. Feel it entering your body and being distributed to every cell. As you exhale, imagine all the tension and accumulated stress leaving your body and being absorbed into the ground. Do this ten times, then rest and relax. When you are ready to stand up, stretch your arms and legs, then stand up slowly.

# coping with stress

**Stress is one of the most common problems in the 21st century. It is caused by the hectic pace at which most of us conduct our lives, with little opportunity to relax or do nothing. We are encouraged to stay in contact with others as much as possible, which can mean being available by mobile phone 24 hours a day. We may feel that we will lose our jobs to a competitive colleague if we take a day off work for a cold or flu, so we struggle on even though our bodies are demanding the time to recover. It is not surprising that many of us end up feeling perpetually tired or vaguely unwell, while others develop physical ailments.**

## blocked chakras

When we allow stress and tension to build up in our bodies, we run the risk of blocking our chakras or stopping them functioning at their best. For instance, if a person habitually stops himself releasing the grief he feels over an unhappy experience, whichever chakra is holding on to that grief will eventually become clogged and sluggish.

The poor state of our chakras soon begins to affect our aura, depleting it so that it too cannot function properly. Eventually, if nothing is done to halt the process, the poor quality of our aura will affect our physical body. The nature of the health problem will depend on where the blockage is in the aura, but it could be anything from depression to cancer.

*This is a single-terminated crystal. It has one pointed and one blunt end. You hold the blunt end and use the point to comb out your chakras.*

## clearing the chakras

You will soon notice a difference if you regularly comb out your chakras. Trust your intuition to tell you which chakras need the most attention, and notice the way you feel as you clean each one. If a chakra is very congested, it might start to feel nicely warm after it has been cleaned, or a symptom related to that chakra may improve or completely vanish.

## combing out the chakras

1  If you want to clear your chakras, whether you know they are blocked or simply as a precautionary measure, you will find it easier if you use a single-terminated quartz crystal. This is a long crystal, one end of which is pointed and the other end blunt. Sit or stand with both feet on the ground, and put yourself into a relaxed and balanced state (see page 31).

2  Hold the crystal by the blunt end, and use the pointed end to comb through your base chakra. Visualize yourself hooking out stagnant energy and blocks from the chakra and putting this into a container. When you are ready, move up to the sacral chakra and repeat the process. Continue working up through the chakras until you have combed out all seven of them. Do not spend more than a couple of minutes on each chakra.

3  Now ask for the energy you have removed to be transformed into energy that can benefit everyone. Leave your crystal in a patch of sunlight or mentally bathe it in white light to cleanse it.

# READING YOUR AURA
# AND ITS COLOURS

When you have learnt to see your aura and those of other people, the next step is to interpret what you can see. Your aura contains a tremendous amount of information about you, from your overall mood and general attitude to the state of your health and your deeply ingrained opinions about yourself. Its shape will be instructive, as you will be able to see if it is evenly balanced all over your body or if it is very small in some places and much larger in others. With practice, you will also be able to discover whether your aura is damaged in places and whether some areas of it are hotter than others.

When you start to examine your own aura, it may solve several mysteries that have always puzzled you about yourself. For instance, you may realize that the colour of your aura is one that you have always loved or which has special significance for you. This is no coincidence, of course; you will have unconsciously responded to this colour because it is in your aura. If you habitually hold a lot of anger in your stomach, you may see or feel this very clearly in the aura around your solar plexus and sacral chakras. As you will discover, your aura is your energetic blueprint.

# what the aura can tell you

**Your aura is an extension of your body, even though you have to train your eyes to be able to see it. As a result, it contains an enormous amount of information about you, all of which is stored in the relevant layer of your aura. For instance, your thoughts are stored in the mental layer of your aura and your feelings belong to the emotional layer.**

## information conveyed by the aura

When someone is very skilled at reading auras, he will appear to read you like a book. That is more or less exactly what he is doing – examining each layer of your aura (see page 21) and seeing what it contains. He will see any blockages that are locked in the mental layer of your aura and how these are affecting you.

For instance, a persistent lack of confidence will be visible in the mental layer, and if it is really ingrained the person will be able to see how it is affecting you emotionally by looking at the emotional layer of your aura. He will then see that this mental block is having a physical effect on your

*Below left: This woman's aura is suffused with areas of muddy, dark green. They show that she is feeling jealous about someone or something.*

*Below right: A bright green aura, such as the one shown here, indicates a peaceful temperament and possible healing ability.*

body, because that will be shown in the etheric template in your aura and also in the chakra nearest the mental block. This chakra might be distorted in some way, such as pushed to one side or torn.

## interpreting what you see

Reading an aura is quite simple but it does take time to master, and learning to interpret what you see can also take time. In Charles Dickens' *A Christmas Carol*, the ghost of Jacob Marley dragged along a chain made from cash-boxes, ledgers and purses, all of which showed his lifelong addiction to making and keeping money. Something similar might be visible in the mental and emotional layers of the aura belonging to someone who has an overriding attachment to financial gain and status symbols. The mental layer will be affected because this person's thoughts continually revolve around money, and the emotional layer will be affected because he has such a powerful emotional need to make and keep money. The etheric layer, which is nearest the body, will inevitably be affected as well and will show how these mental and emotional imbalances have created some form of physical imbalance. You might see all this as clouds of dark, stagnant energy.

## colours

The colours within the aura will also tell you a great deal about a person's mental, emotional and physical state. Generally speaking, bright, clear colours are a positive sign, and dark, muddy colours indicate that something is wrong. You will learn more about the significance of colours in the aura later in this chapter.

## being grounded

With practice, you will be able to tell whether someone is fully grounded and centred in their body, simply by looking at his legs and feet. Does his aura extend all the way down the legs and tuck under the feet, or does it end half way down? If the aura does not wrap around the feet, the person is ungrounded and may have problems with his balance and with his awareness of what is going on around him.

# scanning your aura

**With the help of this book, you will learn how to scan your own aura for important information about yourself. You will gain increased insight into your mental state, your emotions, your physical health and your energy levels.**

Be prepared to amass this information slowly. It is unlikely to arrive overnight, so be patient and be prepared to practise on a regular basis. You may feel that you are not making much progress at first, but do not let this put you off, especially if you often feel discouraged when your first attempts at doing something fail to succeed. You are learning to use your brain, your eyes, your hands and your intuition in new ways, and these take time to master.

*Try scanning your head and face when they are affected by an ailment such as a cold or hay fever. Compare the feel of your aura to the way it is when you are completely healthy.*

You need to build up your expertise slowly by practising the exercises in this book regularly. Stick with them, even when you feel you are not making any progress or you cannot sense your aura. You will eventually succeed if you keep practising; but you never will if you close this book and give up on the whole idea.

## scanning injured areas

One way of learning to tell the difference between the parts of your body that are healthy and those that are not is to scan any problem areas that you know about. For instance, if you have a heavy cold that has completely blocked your sinuses, you could scan your head to see how your aura feels. Does the area around your nose feel different from the rest of your head? Is it heavy or sticky? How does your hand feel as it scans the affected part of your aura? Does it prickle, hurt or feel as though it has got caught in cobwebs? Keep practising, even if you do not feel much at first.

If you cannot sense anything, experiment by slowly moving your hands closer to your face (but not touching it) and then further away again. Is there a point at which you suddenly feel something? Look at yourself in a mirror. Can you see your aura? What does it look like? Turn sideways so you can see the area around your nose. Does it look different from the aura around the rest of your head?

If you have broken a bone or you have a chronic bone problem, such as arthritis, it is very instructive to scan the affected part of your body. Study the aura surrounding it. What does it look like? Can you see any areas of congested energy, or is the colour of your aura here different from the surrounding areas? Compare it with other parts of your body. What does it feel like when you scan it with your hand? Move your hand in and out of your aura until you start to feel something. You may get a mental picture of the area at the same time which will give you valuable information, even if it does not match what you think you should be seeing.

For instance, when scanning a painful joint, you might see long iron nails sticking out of it. This could be puzzling if you know with your rational mind that these nails are not present in the joint, yet the image you get may correspond exactly with the stabbing pains you feel in that joint. If you do see these nails, mentally pull them out and then suffuse the area with golden light.

## scanning plants

Another way to practise scanning auras is to scan those of plants. You can do this quite easily with house plants. Choose a mixture of plants with different leaf shapes, so you can learn for yourself that their auras match the exact outlines of their leaves. Again, you will have to move your hands in and out of a plant's aura until you feel that you have made a connection with it. You can also do this with freshly cut flowers.

When you walk around a garden, you can scan all the plants you see. For instance, you can walk slowly beside a border of plants, holding your outstretched palm above the plants. How does your palm feel? With practice, you will feel as though your palm is being tickled by the leaves on the plants, even though it is not directly in contact with them.

*You can practise scanning auras on plants. Move your hands around the plant until you feel its aura.*

## scanning your aura with your hands

1 One of the easiest ways to scan your aura is with your own hands. This may seem strange at first, but it will soon start to feel more natural and you will learn to let your intuition guide you and to follow your gut instincts. Your hands are very sensitive, especially when you train them to be receptive to what is around them. Choose a time when you will not be disturbed, and sit comfortably with both feet flat on the floor. Put yourself into a relaxed and balanced state (see page 31).

2 Hold your right palm about 5 cm (2 in) above the front of your left arm, or reverse this if you are left-handed. Move your hand slowly through the air above your arm, taking note of any sensations that you register in your scanning palm. When you have finished scanning the front of your arm, scan the back of it. Now scan your left palm. Does it feel any different from the rest of your arm? For instance, can you feel a magnetic pull in the air between your two palms?

3 Move up to your shoulder and across your chest, again registering the sensations you are getting in your right palm. Now slowly scan your trunk, legs and feet. Make a note of any areas that need further attention so you can return to them again later. When you have scanned as much of your body as you can manage with your right hand, use your left hand to scan your right arm and any other areas of your body you could not reach with your right hand. When you have finished, sit quietly for a couple of minutes before standing up.

## scanning your aura visually

**1** Choose a time and place where you can be on your own, then put yourself into a relaxed and balanced state (see page 31). Close your eyes. You can either conjure up an image of your body or mentally look at every area of your body.

**2** Whichever method you choose, the scanning process is the same. Scan your body slowly and systematically, looking for any areas in your aura that look or feel as though they need attention. Trust your instincts and the images that come to you. For instance, you might sense a muddy mass of energy over your stomach that you want to remove, perhaps using the combing out the chakras exercise (see page 53). When you have finished, sit quietly for a couple of minutes before standing up.

# reading your aura

**You need to work systematically when reading your aura or that of another person. Essentially, you need to start at the head and work through to the feet. This will ensure that you do not overlook any areas of the body that may need your attention, especially if you are not aware of them. For instance, you may already know that your feet need to be scanned, but you might not realize that your knees also require some help.**

There are two ways to read your aura. The first is to look at the aura itself (see pages 58–61) and the second is to scan your chakras (see pages 48–49). Ideally, you should do both because together they will give you a complete picture of the state of your aura, but you may find that you prefer one method to the other and that it gives you all the information you need. Keep practising so that you devise a system that works well for you and with which you feel comfortable.

You should never make medical diagnoses based on what you can see or feel in a person's aura. You can identify areas that you think will benefit from attention, but you should never tell someone what you think is physically wrong with them, or pass an opinion about any medication or treatment she is receiving from her doctor. Be equally circumspect when examining your own aura and do not leap to dramatic or frightening conclusions about the state of your health.

## aura shapes

*Opposite, left: The edge of the aura around this person's hand is composed of broken blue blobs. This formation, coupled with the deep purple clouds over the fingers, indicates physical damage to the hand.*

*Opposite, right: This man's aura is lopsided and has been pushed backwards. It must be manipulated back into place.*

Trust your instincts and your intuition when assessing the shape of your aura. Common sense also plays an important role in this, because sometimes the shape of an aura can be read very literally. For instance, if a person's aura feels depressed over his crown chakra, as though it has a big dent in it, it is highly likely that he actually is feeling depressed. Equally, if your hands start to hurt when you reach the aura around his heart, it may mean that he is suffering from heartache.

Here are a few aura shapes you can expect to see and suggestions about what they might mean, as well as how to treat them.

| SHAPE | MEANING | TREATMENT |
|---|---|---|
| Depressed area over crown chakra | Mental depression | Gently tease out the dented part of the aura |
| Lopsided aura | Wariness; fear; lack of trust | Plump up the narrow part and push in the fatter part; auric shield exercise (see page 107) |
| Aura stops at knees | Ungrounded; fear; lack of connection with surroundings | Pull down aura to below the feet; grounding exercise (see page 95) |
| Jagged edge to aura | Lack of boundaries; physical damage to body | Smooth over jagged edges; comb out relevant chakra (see page 53) |

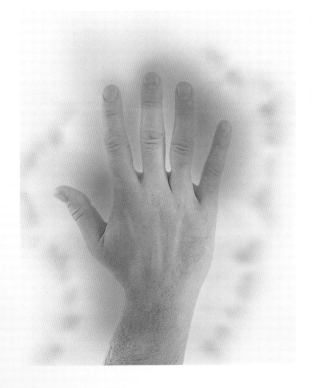

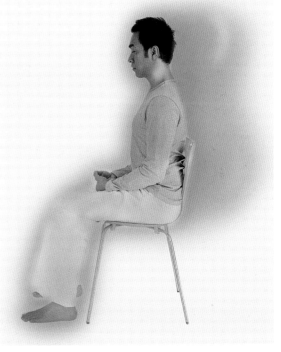

## damage to the aura shapes

Sometimes you will work with auras that have been damaged in some way. For instance, an aura might have tears or holes in it, or you might see that it contains some sort of blockage. You need to repair the damage or remove the blockage, and you may have to repeat the process more than once if the aura has been badly affected.

If you want to remove the blockage, you can do so with your hands. Gently pull the blockage out of the aura and then seal the gap that it has left by imagining it being filled with golden light. Alternatively, you can adapt the chakra-combing exercise (see page 53) and comb out the blockage with a crystal.

*Crystals have powerful energies and are very effective when used to solve problems, such as blockages, in someone's aura.*

| DAMAGE | MEANING | TREATMENT |
|---|---|---|
| *Rips in aura* | *Leaking energy; drug or alcohol abuse* | *Detoxing; grounding exercise (see page 95); repairing rips with hands* |
| *Holes in aura* | *Leaking energy; ill health; damage to chakra* | *Rest; repair chakra with combing exercise (see page 53); smooth over aura to cover holes* |
| *Solid form in aura* | *Energy block; ingrained habits; inflexibility; solid thought form; relationship problems* | *Check colour of block for information about emotions relating to it; removal from aura with hands; cord-cutting (see page 113)* |

## temperature variations in the aura

Sometimes when you scan an aura you will find areas that are much hotter or colder than the rest of the aura. A perfectly healthy aura should be roughly the same temperature throughout, so very hot or cold spots indicate problem areas that need your attention. If you find a hot or cold spot but have not yet experienced a physical problem that corresponds to it, you may be able to ward it off by adjusting the temperature in your aura. Check it daily until it has reverted to the same temperature as the rest of your aura.

*When scanning someone's aura you need to work systematically. It is often most effective to work from the feet up towards the head.*

| TEMPERATURE | MEANING | TREATMENT |
|---|---|---|
| *Hot spot* | *An area that needs healing; a physical problem* | *Comb out the relevant chakra with a crystal (see page 53); smooth over the hot spot with your hands; mentally cover the hot spot with golden light* |
| *Cold spot* | *An area that needs healing; a part of the aura that has been shut off and neglected; relationship problems* | *Practise the cord-cutting exercise (see page 113); clear out stagnant energy from the cold spot with your hands then flood the area with golden light* |

# the colours of life

**Do you have a favourite colour? Do you always enjoy wearing it and do you feel better for having it around you? If so, you already know about the importance of using colour to enhance your life. Equally, there may be some colours that make you feel uncomfortable if you get too close to them or which you cannot wear, even though you may enjoy them when you see them in flowers. Have you ever put on an outfit and then had to take it off again because it felt wrong? If this has happened to you, you have intuitively tuned into your aura and rejected a colour that was temporarily unsuitable for it.**

*Red is not an easy colour to wear. If you can tolerate it, it is very helpful if you want to boost your enthusiasm and competitive spirit.*

We are surrounded by colour in our lives, yet we often have a tendency to take it for granted and not to recognize how important it is to us. It is literally life-enhancing. When prisoners of war were released from captivity after the end of the Second World War, part of their rehabilitation involved being given books of different-coloured pages to look at. When several starving men were given a bowl of cherries, they did not eat them for days because they preferred to gaze at their vivid colours.

## sensing the energy of different colours

This is a lot easier than you may think. The person being scanned, whether it is you or someone else, should either be lying down or sitting in a chair. Simply hold the pendulum or the palm of your hand about 5 cm (2 in) above the relevant area on the front of the body, using the diagram of the major chakras (see pages 42–43). There is no need to touch the person's body.

Pay particular attention to the colours you like best. Can you see them in your aura? Does the depth, strength or colour of your aura change when you wear a specific colour? Do certain colours always affect you emotionally? You can introduce particular colours into your life for specific reasons. For instance, if you are doing a lot of mental work that involves thinking hard, you can wear yellow or have a vase of yellow flowers on your desk to help your thought processes. If you have a sore throat, you can wear a blue scarf to give extra strength to your throat chakra.

## the colours in your aura

Although our auras can change in colour according to our moods and our physical and emotional states, we all have one permanent colour that is always present in our auras. This colour says a lot about us, because it describes our attitudes and beliefs, strengths and weaknesses, and also what we are striving for in life. Marcus Aurelius, the Roman emperor, put it perfectly when he wrote 'The soul becomes dyed with the colour of its thoughts.'

*Place something yellow, such as a vase of flowers, beside you when you need mental inspiration and keep glancing at it.*

When you have discovered which is your own predominant colour you can look it up in the following list. The interpretations given below are suggestions; use your intuition to develop them and to apply them to the people whose auras you are studying. Always trust your intuition and let it guide you to the right interpretation.

## RED

| | |
|---|---|
| **KEY WORDS:** | passion, leadership, competitiveness, physical activity |
| **CHAKRA:** | base |

This is a very vibrant colour to find in someone's aura. It indicates that she is enterprising, dynamic and competitive. This is someone who wants to be first in whatever she does and who enjoys being an innovator. She is a born leader and will hate having to follow in other people's footsteps. She enjoys being active and feels passionately about things; she throws herself head first into life and does not stand on the sidelines. Clear red indicates someone who loves life. A muddy or dull red indicates anger and resentment.

# ORANGE

**KEY WORDS:**    optimism, harmony, confidence, emotional
**CHAKRA:**    sacral

Orange is a wonderfully warm and energizing colour, and someone whose aura is predominantly a clear orange is very positive and confident. This person strides through life, safe in the knowledge that things will go well for her. Sure enough, she always manages to overcome problems and to learn something from them. She is good at mixing with others because she has the warmth and enthusiasm to bring out the best in them. Harsh orange indicates someone who is strident and egotistical. A muddy, dirty orange belongs to someone who is resentful and touchy.

# GREEN

**KEY WORDS:**    love, peace, harmony, healing
**CHAKRA:**    heart

A clear, spring green aura indicates someone who is loving and affectionate, and who instinctively wants to create harmony with others. At times this may make her too eager to please, purely because she wants everyone to be happy. She enjoys being surrounded by nature and needs to be connected to it in order to stay healthy. This person may have a special affinity with animals and an ability to understand them. She also has natural healing powers and may eventually practise some form of healing. A harsh green indicates someone who is stubborn and very resistant to change. A dark, dirty green belongs to someone who is jealous and possessive.

# YELLOW

**KEY WORDS:**     mental abilities, creativity, communication
**CHAKRA:**     solar plexus

When someone has a clear yellow aura, she spends a lot of time in her head, thinking things through. She may or may not be intellectual, but she certainly enjoys using her brain to grapple with ideas and concepts. She is entertaining company and gregarious, and therefore needs to mix with other people. This is not someone who is happy when left on her own for long periods, because she needs to bounce her ideas off others. Acid yellow suggests someone who is very opinionated and believes she is always right. A murky yellow indicates someone who does not always tell the truth.

# PINK

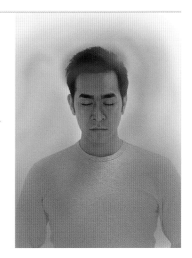

**KEY WORDS:**     love, kindness, spirituality
**CHAKRA:**     heart

When pink is the predominant colour of someone's aura, he is instinctively kind, helpful and affectionate. He is particularly fond of children and animals, and is partly attracted to them because of their innocence and vulnerability. The person is a natural peacemaker and does not enjoy falling out with people. However, he must be careful not to give too much of himself to others, which is what has happened if his aura is a pale, washed-out pink. A hard pink indicates someone who gets carried away by his emotions and who can be sentimental.

## BLUE

**KEY WORDS:**   thoughtful, idealistic, healing, spiritual knowledge
**CHAKRA :**   throat

Blue is the colour that belongs to someone who is idealistic and who has strong beliefs about what is right and wrong. She does her best to live by these rules, even if it means that other people appear to do better in life. She does not care because she knows she is leading her life according to her ethics. She is also a seeker of spiritual knowledge although she wears it lightly. She may practise some form of healing. If her aura is a deep, rich blue, it means she has found her correct path through life and is living out her life's purpose. A dark, dirty blue indicates someone who is conservative and frightened of change.

## PURPLE

**KEY WORDS:**   humanitarian, loving, supportive, psychic ability
**CHAKRA:**   brow

You will see auras in shades of purple from light lilac to rich purple to deep indigo. These are all variations on purple, and they indicate someone who has a strong spiritual purpose and who often has some form of psychic ability, whether or not she is aware of it. She is humanitarian and cares deeply about the fate of others, whether strangers or friends. A clear purple indicates strong psychic ability, whereas a paler purple suggests someone who is intuitive. It is important for anyone whose aura is a shade of purple to be fully grounded as she has a tendency to become disconnected from the world around her and to be too 'airy-fairy'.

# WHITE

KEY WORDS:   spirituality, connection with the Divine
CHAKRA :   crown

You will not often come across someone with a white aura, and when you do you must check that it is not actually pale grey or a very washed-out shade of another colour. Someone with a white aura is spiritually evolved and has a strong connection with the Divine. She is humanitarian, and at times may seem almost too good to be true because she is much more concerned about other people's welfare than her own. It is highly likely that she works with the disadvantaged or with people who have been forgotten by the rest of society. She would certainly be very unhappy in materialistic surroundings. A dirty white aura indicates someone who finds it difficult to connect with others. A very pale white suggests someone who lives in their own world and is divorced from the physical reality around them.

# GOLD

KEY WORDS:   spirituality, higher knowledge, visionary abilities
CHAKRA :   all the chakras

It is very rare to find someone with a golden aura. When you do, you should remember that medieval artists usually portrayed saints with gold haloes around their heads, although it does not automatically mean that you are dealing with a saint. Nevertheless, someone with a gold aura has a tremendous amount of potential and the ability to change the world around him. He also has a deep sense of spirituality and visionary qualities. When someone has a dirty gold aura, it indicates a strong materialistic streak and a desire to wield power.

## SILVER

**KEY WORDS:**    dreams, potential, idealism
**CHAKRA :**    brow

Just as it is rare to find someone with a gold aura, so it is highly unusual to find someone with a silver aura. When you do, it will probably be one of the main colours in her aura rather than the only colour, and sometimes you will see silver streaks or stars. These all represent potential, rather as shooting stars are said to indicate wishes that could come true. For instance, these silver streaks might suggest a baby that is waiting to be conceived or a creative project that has yet to be started. However, the person must take care to turn her potential into reality rather than letting it remain a wonderful dream. Dirty silver streaks in the aura indicate someone who likes to create a sensation.

## GREY

**KEY WORDS:**    camouflage, keeping a low profile
**CHAKRA :**    base

When you find someone with a grey aura, she wants to keep a low profile and not stand out from the crowd. She is adaptable and eager to compromise, which can sometimes mean that she is too amenable for her own good and allows others to impose their own ideas and needs on her. You should check that her grey aura is not caused by health problems and especially by a lack of physical energy. When you see an aura that is a dirty grey, the person may be resentful at being kept in the background and overshadowed by others.

# BROWN

**KEY WORDS:**    solidity, connection with nature, practicality
**CHAKRA :**    base

The owner of a rich brown aura is someone who is practical and down-to-earth, and who has a powerful connection with nature. She enjoys working outdoors and growing plants, or may have a strong desire to protect the environment against harmful influences. A red-brown aura indicates someone who likes to take care of others, and who is ready to fight other people's battles on their behalf. When you find a dirty brown aura, it belongs to someone who is very materialistic and who wants to make sure she gets her own share of whatever is on offer.

# BLACK

**KEY WORDS:**    transformation, change, rest, camouflage
**CHAKRA :**    base

Do not be alarmed if you encounter someone with a black aura, because it is not necessarily a negative sign. It usually indicates that the person wants to hide away from the world and has drawn a protective cloak of invisibility around herself. You should therefore be very careful to ask her permission before examining her aura and be prepared for her to refuse. A black aura, whether it is completely black or there are black streaks in an aura of another colour, can also indicate someone who is physically exhausted and who needs plenty of rest. A thick, dense black can suggest that the person is very needy and draws tremendous amounts of energy from other people.

# CLEANSING YOUR AURA

We need to cleanse our auras, just as we need to clean our homes or wash our bodies. Auras can accumulate a lot of stagnant energy and old emotions that have to be released if they are not to have an adverse effect on us. Very often our auras are able to cleanse themselves, or we release whatever has been held in our auras by instinctively sorting out the situations they relate to. Sometimes, however, our auras need some extra help, especially when we are dealing with long-standing problems or we are under a particular amount of stress.

The exercises in this chapter are all designed to help you to cleanse your aura on a regular basis. Ideally, the process should become as natural to you as brushing your teeth, so that you do it whenever you feel the need. You will soon start to notice a difference, not only physically but also emotionally and mentally. You will realize the importance of cleansing your aura after you have had an unpleasant experience, so you can quickly get rid of any residual energy that has been left in your aura and restore it to a state of balance.

# energy attracts energy

**An aura is a form of energy, in common with everything else in the universe. You may not be able to see your complete aura, and especially not the outer layers, but that does not mean it does not exist. Because it is made of energy, your aura attracts other forms of energy, not all of which are favourable, positive and helpful.**

## how auras retain old emotions and thought patterns

Emotions, especially if they are problematic ones, can get stuck in our auras. This is because we suppress them in an attempt to control them. They then manifest as energy blocks, and after developing your skills at reading auras you may be able to see them. They have a depleting effect on a person's body because the energy in that part of the body is unable to flow properly. Eventually, if these accumulations of energy are not cleared from the aura they will lead to physical ailments and diseases.

It is the same story with repetitive thought patterns, as these will also get lodged in a person's aura. For instance, if someone has spent most of her life believing that she is unintelligent, she will eventually develop an energy block in the aura surrounding her head, perhaps leading to chronic headaches or depression.

## how auras attract other people's emotions

If you have ever felt fit and happy when you went to meet someone but felt ill or drained by the time you said goodbye to him, you will have experienced at first hand what happens when your aura has absorbed another person's emotions. It can feel as though these emotions have enveloped you like a dense cloud and you are unable to shrug them off. You may even feel as though the person has somehow leached the energy out of you. Alternatively, you might wonder why you have started to feel really angry, although you cannot think what you are angry about. If you could see both your auras, you might realize that the other person's aura is leaking anger in your direction, or possibly even sending out little plumes of anger that attach themselves to your aura like burrs to a dog's coat. You really need to cleanse your aura of such debris quickly, before it affects your entire day or even, with repeated exposure, becomes permanently fixed in your aura.

## programming your aura to determine your future

Auras do not only act as magnets to negative or draining blocks of energy, they can also attract positive experiences if we programme them accordingly. This is what happens when someone practises creative visualization or positive thinking: he has actually magnetized his aura to attract the experiences he wants by repeatedly thinking about them. The thought forms that he creates become lodged in his aura and eventually manifest as physical experiences. How often have you heard of someone who has realized a lifelong dream? He managed to do it because, by repeatedly imagining the longed-for situation, he had programmed his aura to attract it.

*We absorb a lot of negative energy from other people when we argue with them. If you have a row with someone and you are still fuming afterwards, it is important for you to cleanse your aura to remove the residual anger.*

# daily auric cleansing

**Very large or dense energy blocks may take a while to vanish from a person's aura, but they will go eventually with repeated cleansing. The best option is not to allow them to accumulate in the first place by following a practice of daily auric cleansing. After all, we wash our bodies every day; so, once we realize that our auras are energetic extensions of our bodies, it makes perfect sense to cleanse them too.**

## why daily cleansing is so important

Think how dirty your clothes can get in a day, especially if you do a lot of travelling or you work in a messy environment. Now imagine how your aura might look at the end of a busy day. It will still hold the residues of the emotions you experienced during the day, such as anger, resentment, frustration or fear. It may also contain unhelpful thought forms, such as anxiety about a loved one or a sense of inferiority, especially if you habitually have these thoughts. Your aura could also contain residues of other people's illnesses or anxieties which they have passed to you during the course of a conversation or even, in some cases, by being in close proximity to them.

You need to get rid of these accumulations of unhelpful thoughts and feelings before they lodge themselves in your aura, eventually leading to long-term problems. The process of cleansing your aura does not take long, so try to get into the habit of doing it at least once a day and more often if you feel you need it. Ideally, you should cleanse your aura at the same time each day so it becomes an established part of your normal routine. You will soon notice the benefits.

In the rest of this chapter, you will find other exercises for specific forms of cleansing which you can use as adjuncts to this daily cleansing exercise.

## daily cleansing

1 Set aside a time when you will not be disturbed. Sit in a chair with both your feet flat on the floor. Put yourself into a balanced and relaxed state (see page 31).

2 Imagine a large disc of energy, much wider than your body, hovering a metre or so (several feet) above the crown of your head.

3 Now imagine the disc slowly moving downwards, passing through your body and aura. As it gradually moves downwards, it will trap all the negative emotions, thoughts and experiences that are caught in your aura. You can either visualize this or, if you are not visually orientated, you can simply know that it is happening.

4 Allow the disc to continue to move slowly downwards until it reaches your feet. The disc will now move through your feet and down into the earth beneath your feet, carrying all the debris in your aura with it. The earth will absorb this debris and cleanse it, before releasing it back into the planet as positive energy.

5 Repeat the exercise if you wish. Then sit quietly for a few moments, with your eyes still closed, before getting up and carrying on with the rest of your day.

# simple cleansing methods

**Here are two simple ways to cleanse your aura when you have experienced a difficult situation and you want to rid yourself of its after-effects as quickly as possible. It only takes a couple of minutes to perform each exercise, especially when you become practised at them, and both will eventually become second nature to you.**

You can perform these exercises in addition to the daily cleansing exercise (see page 79), or do them as and when you need them. For instance, if you have a stressful journey during the rush hour on a hot summer's day or a fraught shopping trip you will feel much calmer if you can cleanse your aura immediately afterwards.

## getting rid of fear or anger

You will also benefit from cleansing your aura after an argument with someone or after you have watched a disturbing film or television programme. The shower of light exercise is particularly good as an emergency measure when you want to cleanse your aura quickly, especially after a shock or some other unpleasant experience. You can follow it up with the daily cleansing exercise if you wish. With practice, you can perform the shower of light exercise anywhere, even in the middle of a crowd or while talking to someone.

The clearing angry energy exercise is excellent for cleansing your aura when you want to work on a specific part of your body, such as your stomach, that always tenses up when you get angry. Ideally, you should perform the exercise when you are alone, even if this means locking yourself in the bathroom for a couple of minutes.

## shower of light

1 Either close your eyes or picture yourself performing the exercise in your mind's eye. The latter option is very useful if you need to keep your eyes open while carrying out the exercise.

2 Imagine a dense shower of golden light raining down on to the crown of your head and cascading over your body. Know that each shining particle of light is helping to clean your aura by carrying away negative energy.

3 Imagine the golden light soaking into the ground deep beneath your feet where it will be absorbed by the planet and transformed into positive, healing energy.

## clearing angry energy

1 Try to perform this exercise as soon after the annoying experience as possible, before the anger is absorbed into your body. If you already know which area of your body you want to work on, go straight to it. If not, scan your aura with your hands (see pages 58–61) until you find an area that feels hot, heavy or tangled.

2 With your hands, tease out the congested energy in the relevant part of your aura. As you work, picture yourself pulling the energy out of your aura and depositing it in a special receptacle. The process may trigger particular memories or emotions, so allow yourself to feel them; this exercise is about letting go. When you have removed the energy, smooth down your aura with your hands and ask for the discarded energy to be transformed into beneficial energy.

# auric brushing

**We brush our hair to keep it in good condition and we can brush our auras for the same reason. Auric brushing is a very useful technique to add to your repertoire, and it can come in particularly handy when you are feeling tired or depressed. It only takes a couple of minutes to perform the exercise (see below), so it is a quick way to refresh yourself.**

When you brush your aura, you are removing dirt and debris from it with your hands, just as you would use your hands to brush dust or sand off your clothes. It is a very simple process, but you must be careful about how you dispose of the energy that you are removing from your aura.

## getting rid of the energy

You cannot simply drop the energy you brush out of your aura onto the floor because it will stay there and you will probably reabsorb it before it has been transformed into positive energy. The best option is to deposit the energy in an imaginary container and, when you have finished, ask for that energy to be transformed so it becomes beneficial. You can then picture it being released into the atmosphere for everyone's benefit.

## how to sharpen your mental focus

If you are feeling muzzy-headed and sluggish at a time when you need a sharp mental focus, such as before an important meeting, you can work on reshaping the aura around your head (see opposite). If you wish, you can see what happens to your aura while performing this exercise by looking in a mirror. You will see that any lumps or uneven patches in your aura will be smoothed out, and if it is lopsided you will have brushed it into a more regular shape.

# brushing your aura with your hands

1 Stand up straight, with both feet flat on the ground. Using the palms of your hands, begin to brush the aura around your head and shoulders in long, downward-sweeping movements. Work systematically in sections, each time gathering up the discarded energy in your hand and placing it in an imaginary container that you have put in a convenient position.

2 Continue to work in systematic sections around your aura, sweeping the aura around your left arm with your right hand and then reversing the process. Sweep down the aura around the back and front of your trunk and down your legs. Do not forget to brush the aura around your feet.

3 If any areas of your aura feel heavy, sticky or strange, return to them and continue to brush them until they feel better. When you have finished, ask for the discarded energy in the container to be transformed into beneficial energy.

# reshaping the aura around your head

1 Find a place where you can be alone. If you wish, you can stand in front of a mirror. Place both hands, palms innermost, above the crown of your head and move them downwards in the air, as though you are smoothing down your hair. Discard the energy in an imaginary container.

2 Repeat this process all around your head in flowing movements. As you do this, you may feel a tickling sensation on the top of your head as your crown chakra (see page 41) is activated. Look in the mirror to see the aura around your head change shape.

# scanning and mending

**As you become used to working with your aura, you can progress to more complicated techniques, such as checking your aura for damage. When you perform the techniques described here you must give your intuition full rein, especially if you are not yet able to see what you are doing. Remember the importance of believing in what you are doing and in trusting that it is having a beneficial effect on your aura.**

*Use a mirror to examine the aura around your face and head. Remember to look at your face from more than one angle so you get a better view of your aura.*

If you get into the habit of scanning your aura on a regular basis, whether daily or weekly, you will be able to monitor your health and will even be able to ward off minor ailments, such as sore throats or colds, before they become fully established.

## looking for tears in your aura

As well as using the scanner to detect tears in your aura, you can also give your aura a visual check. This is an advanced technique that you can use when you are able to see the aura all around your body. Alternatively, you can use your mind's eye to scan your aura. It all depends on which method works best for you and feels most natural.

Look at each section of your body in turn, using a mirror to examine your head. Can you see any tears or other damage to your aura? If so, it is important to mend them as soon as possible, because the damage will have a weakening effect on your aura and this will eventually be translated to your body. The tears and rips in your aura are also places where other people's energy can have an adverse effect on you. If you find any tears or areas of damage, do not panic. You can mend them using the scanning exercise below. Repeat it on a daily basis, if not more often, until all the damage has been repaired.

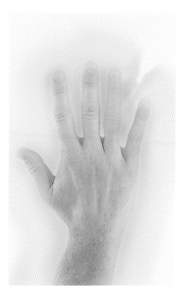

*There is a noticeable gap in the aura surrounding this person's ring and little fingers, suggesting a physical problem in this area.*

## using the scanner to mend your aura

1 When performing this exercise, you can either lie flat or sit in a comfortable chair. Choose a time when you will not be disturbed. Close your eyes and put yourself into a relaxed and balanced state (see page 31). Now imagine that you are lying on a four-poster bed made of metal. A square piece of machinery is positioned high above your head. This is the scanner.

2 When you are ready, imagine the scanner starting to move very gradually down towards your feet. Hear the gentle noise it makes as it slowly scans your aura, looking for tears and other damage. Know that it will repair these tears and mend any other damage as soon as it finds it, without any input from you. Relax and feel the scanner doing its work.

3 When the scanner reaches your feet, it will stop briefly and then begin moving back towards your head. As it moves, know that it is carrying out a second scan of your aura. If you feel discomfort in a part of your body, know that the scanner will pay particular attention to the corresponding section of your aura.

4 When the scanner has reached your head again, it will stop moving. Rest for a few seconds, then imagine yourself standing up and feeling refreshed.

*A singing bowl utilizes the powerful healing properties of sound to cleanse your aura.*

# other cleansing methods

**So far we have looked at ways in which you can cleanse, scan and mend your aura by working with it directly or on a psychic level. We are now going to look at other methods of cleansing your aura, all of which use physical objects. Methods such as singing bowls and crystals work powerfully at an energetic level, even though they seem very simple.**

All the cleansing methods described here are excellent for clearing your aura of negative energy, especially if you feel you have been contaminated by an unpleasant experience or uncomfortably influenced by someone. Ideally, you should combine one or more of these methods with some of the exercises described on pages 79 and 81. Allow your intuition to tell you which is the most appropriate exercise to choose.

## a singing bowl

Sound has very cleansing properties. Originally this is why bells were rung during religious and sacred ceremonies: they were used to cleanse the atmosphere of any stagnant or disruptive energy. They still perform this function today, even though this aspect of bell-ringing may have been long forgotten in many cultures.

The resonance created by a singing bowl has a special quality because the sound is so clear, pure and high. The bowls, which are made from various types of metal, can be bought from shops or via the internet. It is best to visit a shop that offers a selection of bowls and to choose the one with the tone that most appeals to you. This is a very personal matter, so it is not a good idea to let another person choose your bowl for you.

To use a singing bowl, place it on a flat surface, such as a table or floor, and hit its rim with the beater. The sound will swell before gradually dying away, and if you hold your hands over the bowl you will be able to feel the vibrations in the air caused by the ringing of the bowl.

To cleanse your aura using a singing bowl, sit quietly beside it and then strike its side with the beater. You can strike the bowl a few more times to create an intensity of sound, then sit still and feel the waves of sound washing over you. If you want to concentrate on a particular part of your body, such as your hip, position it closest to the bowl so it can fully absorb the vibrations of sound. You may need a friend to help you with this. You should also be careful about putting your ears too close to the bowl when you are ringing it very loudly.

## crystals

These are an excellent way of cleansing your aura's energy, and you can buy them from many conventional shops as well as specialist outlets that stock more unusual crystals. Just as singing bowls are very personal choices, you should select a crystal on the basis of how it feels to you. You must feel attracted to it.

You can use several different crystals for auric cleansing. If you want to concentrate on a particular chakra (see pages 40–41), you should choose

*Specific crystals can cleanse particular chakras. Rose quartz is ideal for the heart chakra.*

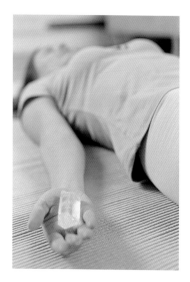

*Some crystals cannot be cleansed in water because it will damage them. Instead, they can be cleansed by imagining that they are being showered with white light.*

a crystal that is the same colour as that chakra. You will find a list of these in the next chapter (see page 99). You can wear the crystal next to your skin or meditate with it. Alternatively, if you want to work on all your chakras, you can use a clear quartz, because this contains the entire spectrum of light and therefore each of the chakra colours.

A simple exercise with a rock crystal is to hold it in your cupped hands and imagine white light pouring down onto it, cleansing it of all negativity. Then, when you are ready, sit or lie quietly with the crystal on a flat surface beside you. Imagine all the negative energy in your aura being transmitted to the crystal. Know that this is happening even if you cannot feel it. When you feel better, imagine the crystal being cleansed with white light again, so it is purged of all your negative energy.

## salt baths

If you ever feel that you have been contaminated by someone's energy, you can cleanse your aura with a salt-water bath. Pour a generous handful of rock salt crystals into an empty bath and then fill it with hot water, as you would for an ordinary bath. Lie in the bath, with the water up to the level of your ears, for about 20 minutes. Get out of the bath, pull the plug and, as you watch the water swirling away, know that it is taking all the debris from your aura with it. Dry yourself with a clean towel and relax in a chair for a few minutes while drinking a large glass of mineral water.

*Never underestimate the power of water to cleanse your aura. One option is to put some sea salt in your bath water. Another is to go for a swim in the sea.*

## bach flower remedies

There are 38 different Bach flower remedies. Each one is made from mineral water impregnated with the energy of a beneficial plant, tree or flower and then preserved in brandy. These remedies work at an energetic level, bringing our emotions and thoughts back into balance and then transferring the balanced energy to our physical bodies. Their beauty lies in their simplicity and effectiveness. They are sold in pharmacies, health food shops and via the internet.

Several of the flower remedies are particularly effective for auric cleansing. Crab Apple is the best remedy if you want to give your aura a general 'spring clean'. Walnut is excellent if you feel uncomfortably influenced or dominated by another person. White Chestnut is ideal if you are haunted by persistent, repetitive thoughts. Each remedy will gently cleanse your aura and restore it to a balanced state. Choose the remedy according to the way you are feeling at the time, rather than how you used to feel or how you want to feel in the future.

You can use a Bach flower remedy in one of several ways. You can add four drops to a glass of water and sip it as required until you feel better, or put four drops in your bath water. Alternatively, you can make up a treatment bottle (see below), especially if you want to take one or more of the remedies over an extended period.

*Bach flower remedies are preserved in brandy. If you are unable to swallow even minute amounts of alcohol, you can add the remedies to your bath water or rub them into your skin instead.*

## preparing a bach flower remedy

1 You can combine up to seven remedies at any one time, but you should only choose the ones you need. Buy a 30 ml stopper bottle from a pharmacy, and add two drops of each of your chosen remedies. Fill up the bottle with still mineral water. This is your treatment bottle.

2 Take four drops from your treatment bottle at least four times a day until you feel better. Usually, you will know that you no longer need the remedy because you will have forgotten to take it.

3 If new feelings arise during the treatment, choose the appropriate remedy and add two drops to your treatment bottle.

# STRENGTHENING YOUR AURA

Think of your aura as a bubble of energy that encloses your body and chakras within its strong protective shield. Although it is very efficient at warding off negative influences and harmful energies, nevertheless there are times when it needs to be strengthened to increase its protective abilities. The exercises in this chapter will help you to boost the resilience of your aura without closing yourself off to any beneficial influences that you want to receive, such as love from other people. You will also discover how to take care of your aura by avoiding or reducing your exposure to many of the forms of pollution that surround us in the 21st century, including electromagnetic currents.

Apparently simple activities, such as eating a healthy diet, drinking alcohol in moderation, taking plenty of exercise, enjoying positive relationships and living with loving pets are all excellent ways of strengthening and protecting your aura. They will also have a beneficial impact on your body, your emotional health and your state of mind, all of which are intimately connected with your aura.

# why you need to strengthen your aura

Although our auras are fairly resilient to outside forces, they still need to be strengthened and protected. Many of the things that can affect our auras are man-made products of our 21st-century society, such as electromagnetic pollution. Our auras can also be badly affected by other people's negative energy, and by hectic schedules with not enough time for decent rest and recuperation. These all have the potential to undermine our health, first by affecting our auras and then by affecting our physical bodies.

## energy-sapping people

Some people are energy-enhancers; we feel better for being with them. Others are energy-sappers; we feel good when we first see them and they are usually feeling miserable, and by the time we say goodbye to them the roles have been reversed. We walk away feeling exhausted and probably worried about them, and they disappear feeling rejuvenated and a lot more cheerful. This does not make them bad people, simply needy both

*The technological revolution has transformed our lives but has also dramatically increased the amount of electromagnetic pollution in the air around us.*

emotionally and energetically. You do not need to cut them out of your life, unless your relationship is so unbalanced and demanding that it is making you ill (even then, it may be impossible to sever all connections with them, perhaps because they are blood relatives). You simply need to make yourself more resilient to them by strengthening your aura.

## energetic pollution

The air we breathe is full of electromagnetic frequencies. These are so new that research is still being conducted into how they affect us, but there are already heated debates about the impact that power lines, pylons and mobile phone masts have on us. Even in the average home you will find televisions, computers, cordless telephones, refrigerators and freezers that all emit electromagnetic frequencies and which therefore have an effect on our auras.

Most of us do not want to live without these modern inventions, but at least we can protect ourselves from their potentially harmful effects by taking care of our auras. Doing so can be as simple as switching off our computers when we have finished using them for the day and unplugging their electrical sockets; some authorities believe that electrical appliances will emit harmful frequencies even when switched off if they are still connected to a power supply.

*One of the simplest ways to keep healthy and to flush toxins through our systems is to drink plenty of clean, fresh water each day.*

## life in the fast lane

A busy life can be exciting and stimulating, but it can also take its toll on our health. Too many late nights, not enough sleep and meals snatched on the run can all deplete our energy and, therefore, weaken our auras. Many of us are also dehydrated for much of the time, perhaps because we do not get enough opportunities during the day to drink plenty of fluids or because we choose drinks that act as diuretics and therefore flush water out of our systems.

A combination of these factors can seriously deplete our energy over time, although we may get so used to feeling tired that we have forgotten what it feels like to be completely healthy. When we feel like this, we definitely need to give our auras a helping hand.

# using your aura to stay grounded

**Being grounded means keeping a solid connection with the planet beneath our feet. This enables us to draw up energy from the earth, which rejuvenates us and keeps us healthy.**

However, being grounded is important for another reason, especially if you want to train yourself to see and read auras. If you are grounded, with your aura firmly anchored in the earth, you will be able to achieve greater success when using your intuition and psychic abilities than if you are ungrounded. You will have better powers of discretion, telling you whether your instincts are correct, and you will also find it easier to forge firm links with the spirit realms and then return to your everyday life afterwards.

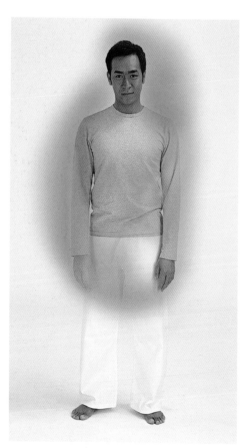

*This man's aura stops at his knees, which shows that he is not grounded. In addition, his aura is lopsided around his head and should be pushed back into place.*

## how to tell if you are ungrounded

There are some easy ways to tell if you are ungrounded. You will feel light-headed and dizzy, especially if you stand up quickly or bend down too suddenly. Your feet might be cold even though the rest of you is warm. You could suffer from repeated colds or other minor ailments, or feel drained most of the time. Another classic sign of being ungrounded is when you attract a lot of static electricity for no apparent reason.

## simple ways to ground yourself

The grounding exercise will help you to ensure that you are grounded, and will strengthen the connections you already have with the earth. Practise it every day, or whenever you feel the need to reconnect yourself with the earth. For instance, if you are badly intimidated by someone or you experience a sudden shock, you could tear your grounding roots. You will then have to 'grow' new ones as quickly as possible. With practice, that will be very easy.

Sometimes, however, you need to do something more to ground yourself. If you feel ungrounded despite the grounding exercise, it may be because your aura has retracted from your feet and now ends somewhere around your knees. Look at the aura around your legs to see if this has happened. If so, all you need do is to get hold of where your aura ends and tug it downwards until it tucks under your feet.

## grounding yourself

1 Sit on an upright chair with both feet flat on the floor. If this is not possible for some reason, simply imagine that your feet are on the floor. Let your hands lie loosely in your lap. Relax by breathing deeply in and out several times.

2 Imagine that your feet are very large and that long roots are growing out of the soles of your feet deep into the earth. Picture them moving downwards, branching out into still more roots, until an entire network of roots is connecting you with the energy of the planet. Your feet will start to feel heavier and warmer. They may also tingle.

3 Picture the roots reaching the centre of the earth. Now breathe deeply, feeling the earth's energy moving up the roots into your feet with each inhalation. Feel this energy flowing into your body, from your feet to the top of your head, until it is completely filled. Sit quietly for a couple of minutes, stretch your arms and legs, and then stand up.

# energizing your aura

**A healthy aura means a healthy person. An unhealthy or damaged aura will eventually lead to some form of illness because the person is being deprived of energy and vitality. He may even have holes in his aura through which energy is draining away. Such damage to a person's aura must be repaired, and then he can follow the methods described here to boost his aura again.**

## keeping the aura vibrant and healthy

It does not take much to keep our auras in good condition. We need to lead balanced lives, in which we combine productive forms of activity with periods of rest and recuperation. Of course, there are occasions when most of us feel stressed and anxious, and when the balance of our lives is upset for some reason, but we normally recover quickly when the status quo is restored.

*Our auras reflect our state of health. We place our bodies under tremendous strain if we do not eat a balanced diet containing plenty of fruit and vegetables.*

Fresh air is essential, because it enables us to clear our lungs of pollutants and fully oxygenate our blood. Many of us are shallow breathers, never properly filling our lungs with air and therefore never properly expelling the stale air either. Exercise is also a must, even if it is as simple as taking a short walk each day. Flogging yourself into an early grave by taking too much exercise, however, will deplete your aura and put your body under great stress.

No one would expect a car to perform well without petrol or diesel, yet many of us expect to lead high-powered lives while eating food with poor nutritional value. Advocates of organic food claim it gives them many health benefits, but it is expensive and not everyone can afford it. Yet even increasing the amount of ordinary fruit and vegetables you eat each day, and ensuring your body is hydrated by drinking plenty of water, will have a big impact on your aura and, therefore, on your health.

## laughter is the best medicine

Another way to energize your aura is to have a good laugh on a daily basis. There have been scientific studies into the effectiveness of laughter, and in some cases people have claimed that regular bouts of mirth have saved their lives by curing terminal illnesses. Laughter opens up our lungs, massages our diaphragms and boosts our immune systems, as well as making us feel great.

*Walking barefoot along a beach is a marvellous way to revitalize our auras and cleanse them at the same time.*

## invigorating the aura

1  This is a great exercise for when you feel tired but there is not enough time for a proper rest. Stand with your feet slightly apart and flat on the floor. Breathe deeply in and out for a couple of minutes to relax yourself completely.

2  Bend forwards and scoop up the aura in front of your feet. Lift it up in both hands and place it on top of your head. Now repeat the exercise to the right and left of your feet. Finally, reach behind you to scoop up the aura at the back of your feet and lift it as high as you can manage. You will immediately feel more invigorated and alert.

# boosting your aura with crystals

**Crystals are powerful energizers. Even small crystals no bigger than your thumbnail contain a surprising amount of energy that you can use to boost and protect your aura. All you need to do is to choose one or more crystals that feel right for you and to start working with them. Although you will find lots of suggestions here for ways to use your crystals, you should also follow your own intuition and be prepared to experiment.**

## choosing a suitable crystal

The first step is to find a crystal that feels good to you, and which you feel you can work with. Although you can buy crystals via the internet and by mail order, it is much better to choose your own crystals in a shop, where you can see and feel them.

Always trust your instincts when selecting a crystal. You might be shown the most beautiful, flawless crystal in the shop and be told that it is perfect for strengthening your aura, but you should not buy it if you do not like the way it feels when you hold it. It might make you feel uncomfortable or nervous, or it might even make your hand ache. Choose a crystal that you feel drawn to, and which feels good when you hold it. Sometimes a crystal seems to jump into your hand when you get near it, and this is an excellent way of selecting the perfect crystal for you.

If you have time and the shop is not too crowded, you can scan a crystal's aura (see page 100) to ensure it is suitable for you. Alternatively, you can buy a crystal that you know you like and scan it when you get home.

## crystals for strengthening your aura

If you want to work with a particular chakra (see pages 40–41) you can choose a crystal of the same colour. Therefore, if you want to strengthen your solar plexus chakra, which is traditionally associated with the colour yellow, you should choose a yellow crystal, such as yellow citrine. However, if you wish to strengthen all your chakras, or you are still learning to tune into them, you could choose a clear quartz crystal. This is a good choice because white contains every colour of the spectrum. Tourmaline is another excellent option.

## THE CHAKRAS AND CRYSTALS

| | | |
|---|---|---|
| **BASE CHAKRA** | *Dark brown and red crystals such as garnet, reddish amber, ruby, bloodstone and black tourmaline* | |
| **SACRAL CHAKRA** | *Orange crystals such as coral, carnelian, orange calcite, sardonyx and topaz* | |
| **SOLAR PLEXUS CHAKRA** | *Yellow crystals such as yellow citrine, amber, golden calcite, aventurine and tiger's eye* | |
| **HEART CHAKRA** | *Pink and green crystals such as rose quartz, pink calcite, rhodochrosite, malachite, green calcite and emerald* | |
| **THROAT CHAKRA** | *Blue crystals such as sapphire, aquamarine, turquoise, blue topaz and blue lace agate* | |
| **BROW CHAKRA** | *Indigo and purple crystals such as amethyst, lapis lazuli, azurite, charoite and sodalite* | |
| **CROWN CHAKRA** | *Violet and white crystals such as iolite, diamond, clear calcite, clear quartz, herkimer and moonstone* | |

*You can boost your aura by wearing a crystal next to your skin. This jade pendant has been specially chosen to enhance the woman's heart chakra, which is associated with the colour green.*

## increasing your aura's strength with crystals

One of the easiest ways to strengthen your aura is to wear your chosen crystal next to your skin every day, or to carry it in one of your pockets so you can handle it whenever you wish. Alternatively, you can place the crystal beside your bed at night, so you can absorb its energies while you sleep, or have it near you during the day while you work. Rose quartz is especially effective at counteracting the harmful effects of electromagnetic pollution, so it is a good choice to place beside your computer or television set.

You can also choose a suitable crystal for each chakra and then lie down with the relevant crystal balanced on each chakra. You will have to place the crystal for your crown chakra beside your head. Lie quietly and know that your chakras are absorbing the energies they need from the crystals. When you are ready to get up, carefully remove all the crystals and spend a couple of minutes coming back into your body. It is a good idea to ground yourself (see page 95) after the exercise.

## cleansing the crystals after use

Crystals absorb energy and can quickly get clogged with negative energy. Some crystals can be soaked in water without coming to any harm, but others will dissolve when given this treatment. If you are unsure whether it is safe to wash your crystal, you can mentally bathe it in white light instead, while asking for it to be cleansed and then leave it in a sunny place for several hours to recharge its energies.

## sensing a crystal's aura

1 Activate your hand chakras (see page 47) if you are unused to sensing objects with your hands. Hold the palms of your hands above the crystal and tune into its energies.

2 Note how the crystal feels to you. Can you feel a slight coolness wafting up from it or a sense of warmth? Does it have any other physical impact on you? Do you like how it feels? Let your instincts tell you whether this is a good crystal for you and whether you should buy it or leave it in the shop.

# recharging your aura

1 You will need two single-terminated crystals for this exercise. A single-terminated crystal is pointed or terminated at one end and blunt at the other. Clear quartz crystals are ideal for this exercise because they are suitable for healing all sorts of ailments as well as for recharging your aura, making them extremely versatile. Sit in an upright chair with both feet on the ground, then put yourself into a relaxed and balanced state (see page 31).

2 Hold a crystal in each hand. Make sure the terminated end of the crystal is pointing towards your wrist in your left hand and the terminated end of the crystal in your right hand is pointing towards your fingers, so the energy flows properly.

3 Close your eyes. Ground yourself (see page 95) and imagine a silver cord is connecting your crown chakra with the spirit realms. Now breathe in, knowing the crystal in your left hand is drawing in energy and circulating it around your aura. Breathe out, knowing the stale energy is being expelled through the crystal in your right hand. This is one cycle. Repeat this exercise for at least nine more cycles or until your aura feels stronger. Then sit quietly for a couple of seconds before grounding yourself again and coming back into your body.

# using your breath to strengthen your aura

**Breath is the life force of every living creature and plant on the planet. If we do not breathe, we die; it is as simple as that. As we humans breathe in, we take in oxygen though our inflating lungs. This passes into our blood, which distributes the oxygen to all the cells in our bodies. As we breathe out, we expel carbon dioxide waste from our deflating lungs, where it has collected. This is a perfect system and for most of the time we are unaware of it taking place.**

## shallow breathing

Most babies breathe perfectly. As we get older, however, we learn all sorts of behaviour that interferes with our once-perfect breathing. We may start to slouch, so we contract our lungs and never give them the chance to inflate and deflate properly. We may become tense, so we unconsciously hold our breath and, in doing so, restrict our breathing. Or we might breathe in a very shallow fashion, only using the top sections of our lungs.

All these, and other bad breathing habits, reduce the amount of oxygen that enters our bodies and the amount of carbon dioxide that is expelled from them. As a result, we feel tired and listless. Our digestion may be sluggish. Our skin may become pallid or spotty. If we become injured or ill, it can take a long time for our bodies to recover because our blood is not fully oxygenated.

## the effect on our auras

Failure to breathe properly has a direct impact on our auras: shallow or restricted breathing leads to a depleted and narrow aura. You can see this for yourself if you observe the depth of your aura while taking shallow breaths, and then watch it again while taking deep breaths. Your aura will increase considerably when you breathe properly. As a result of the increased size of your aura, your general energy levels will dramatically improve, your immune system will be boosted and your digestive system will function more efficiently.

Practise the breath of life exercise once a day. However, if you suffer from a medical condition, especially high blood pressure, you should check with your doctor first.

## the breath of life

1 Either sit comfortably with both feet on the floor or lie flat on the floor (but not a bed). Close your eyes and place your hands on either side of your navel. Relax.

2 Place the tip of your tongue on the soft ridge of tissue just above the back of your two front teeth. You will keep it here throughout the exercise. Now breathe in slowly to a count of five. Feel the air filling the top third of your lungs, then the middle section of your lungs and finally flowing into the bottom third of your lungs. By now your abdomen should be inflated, with increased space between your two hands.

3 Hold your breath to a count of five, then gently breathe out to a count of five. Feel your lungs compressing, your abdomen shrinking and your hands moving closer together as you do this.

4 Begin the cycle again. Inhale to a count of five, hold your breath to a count of five and exhale to a count of five. Repeat for a further eight cycles and then relax.

*Research is still being conducted into the effects of mobile phones on their users. You could carry out your own experiment by observing your aura while using your mobile phone. Can you see any changes to your aura?*

# protecting your aura from electronic pollution

**We would be astonished if we could see the number of electromagnetic fields in the air around us. Although we may not be able to avoid these electromagnetic fields completely, we can at least reduce our exposure to them.**

Some of these solutions are very simple. For instance, you could switch off your mobile phone when it is not in use. When it is switched on, do not have it in direct contact with your body but carry it in a bag instead. When you use a landline, opt for a telephone where the handset is connected to the base by a cord. A cordless handset transmits radio waves to and from its base station, so it acts in a similar way to a mobile phone.

## combating electromagnetic frequencies

One of the most effective ways of countering electromagnetic frequencies is to put as much distance between us and an electrical appliance as possible. Most of us use computers in some form or other, whether for business or pleasure. They are almost unavoidable, but we can at least reduce the impact they have on us energetically. Sit back from your computer, rather than hunched over it. When buying a computer screen, choose one with reduced electromagnetic emissions. Switch your computer off when you are not using it, rather than leaving it in sleep mode, or at least move away from it and sit in another part of the room. Whenever you work in a confined space with a computer, open the window. A little fresh air will dramatically help to improve the atmosphere around you.

Do not leave your television, radio, DVD player or similar pieces of equipment on standby, which uses up surprising amounts of electricity, when they are not in use: switch them off completely. Avoid sleeping next to a plug-in clock radio and swap your electric blanket for a hot-water bottle or warmer bedclothes.

Plants can combat electromagnetic frequencies. Place a spider plant (*Chlorophytum comosum*) or a peace lily (*Spathyphyllum wallisii*) near your computer or television to absorb some of its electromagnetic emissions. Buy a piece of rose quartz and leave it on your desk near your computer terminal. Finally, practise the spiral of light exercise (see below) on a regular basis to clean your aura of any residual electromagnetic pollution.

*Placing a spider plant near your computer will not only make your desk look more decorative but will help your body to cope with electromagnetic emissions.*

## spiral of light

1 Put yourself in a relaxed and balanced state (see page 31). If possible, stand outside in natural light but away from electrical appliances. If indoors, choose a room filled with as few electrical appliances as possible and make sure they are all switched off. Stand up, with your arms hanging loosely by your sides and close your eyes.

2 Imagine a huge spiral of golden light spinning above your head. See it flickering with life and energy. Now imagine it moving downwards until it envelops your entire body and aura.

3 Feel it spinning around you very rapidly, removing all electromagnetic pollution from your aura as it does so. Feel it gradually moving downwards until it starts to disappear into the floor beneath your feet, taking the pollution with it so that it can be transformed into beneficial energy.

4 Stand quietly for a few seconds, breathing gently, then make sure you are grounded (see page 95) before opening your eyes.

# protecting your aura
# in difficult situations

**So far we have discussed how to protect your aura from electromagnetic pollution, but there are times when it is necessary to protect it from other hazards as well, such as a threatening atmosphere or someone's negative attitude.**

The number of times you will want to protect your aura will vary according to the life you lead and the people you meet along the way. If you have a very busy or stressful job in which you encounter difficult people on a regular basis, you might want to protect your aura before starting each day, and to check it during the day to make sure all your protective measures are still in place. Alternatively, you may only want to protect your aura when you feel scared or uneasy, or when spending time with someone who always drains your energy.

## practice makes perfect

*The solar plexus chakra is a very sensitive part of the aura. It is always a good idea to protect it with a circle of white light before meeting people who you know will drain you or when dealing with difficult situations.*

As you will discover, it is easy to erect a protective barrier around your aura, and with practice it will only take a couple of seconds to surround yourself with a protective shield. The key is to keep practising, especially at first when the entire process is new to you. Take note of how you feel with the protective shield in place, and whether it makes other people behave differently towards you. Are they less aggressive, or do they complain that you are not as easy to talk to as you used to be? Do you find it easier to stand up to these people and not to be taken for granted by them? Do you feel less affected or influenced by them?

## protecting your solar plexus chakra

The solar plexus chakra (see page 40), which is located just below the sternum, is the seat of our emotions. It can easily become overloaded with unprocessed emotions, especially if we are with people who drain us or who need our help. This chakra can soak up other people's misery and neediness, and then hold it all like a sponge. If all these emotions are not regularly cleared out of the chakra, their build-up can lead to stomach ailments or other physical problems. Once you have cleared your solar plexus of these unprocessed emotions (see page 53), you can protect this chakra when necessary by mentally wrapping a belt of white light around your waist.

## creating an auric shield

1  If possible, sit quietly for a couple of seconds so you are in a relaxed state. Cleanse your aura using your preferred visualization method. Imagine that your aura is being surrounded by a protective, egg-shaped shield. See this shield encasing your aura from above your head to beneath your feet. Make sure it meets around your back, so there are no holes or gaps.

2  Know that this auric shield will protect you from negative influences by repelling them, but that it will allow positive emotions, thoughts and influences to penetrate the shield and reach you. Also know that your positive emotions and thoughts can flow through your shield towards other people, so you are not cut off from them.

3  From time to time throughout your day, check that your shield is in place by visualizing it. Is it intact? You can re-create it if you think it has vanished.

# YOUR AURA AND YOUR RELATIONSHIPS

Love is a vital life force, and no one can survive without some form of it. When healthy babies are deprived of all expressions of love, they give up the will to live. In this chapter you will learn the influence that your aura has on your relationships, and what happens to it when you are in contact with people that you love and those that you are not so keen on.

You will also discover how to work with a partner to strengthen the auric connection between you by playing with one another's auras. As you do this, you will increase your ability to tune into other people's auras and therefore become more sensitive to them. You can also practise on your pets by stroking their auras rather than their bodies. Cats in particular react to this very well and often start purring loudly. You will also find them watching your hands, as though they can see your aura and the way it is interacting with theirs. While doing all this, you need to trust your intuition and know that it is guiding you in the right direction.

# the forces of attraction

**Why do we find some people attractive while being repelled by others? Often this reaction seems inexplicable, especially when encountering someone who is a perfect stranger. You do not know this person; yet you may feel very drawn to them, or you may want to put as much distance between the two of you as possible. Why is that?**

*When you are with someone whose company you enjoy, your aura will extend towards that person's, and vice versa. You may also have very similar auras, which accounts for the easy familiarity between you.*

If you could look at the energy being exchanged between you, all would be revealed. When you feel an immediate attraction towards someone, it is because your auras are very similar in colour and shape. You therefore feel at home with this person because you have a lot in common on an energetic level. Alternatively, when you feel alienated by someone, it is because there is an incompatibility between your auras. Perhaps one person's aura is pushing towards the other's, which immediately goes into full retreat. Or the other person's aura may be very murky and muddy, so you instinctively want to keep your distance.

## long-standing relationships

Couples who have been happily together for a long time often have auras that are very similar to each other. You will also see many energetic links flowing between the two auras, especially linking the two heart chakras. Occasionally, when two people enjoy an extremely close relationship, both emotionally and mentally, their two auras quickly merge whenever they are near each other. You will be able to see this for yourself if you ask them for permission to view their auras when they are together. Do remember that you must always ask a person's permission before looking at his aura, otherwise you are prying into very private areas that are none of your business.

## how we attract what we send out

Have you ever noticed how your moods can be catching? If you feel grumpy and cross, soon the people around you feel the same. If you feel cheerful and happy, everyone else can soon follow suit. That is because we tend to attract what we send out. So, if you are sending out grumpy feelings, you will normally start to receive them before too long.

Sometimes, if you encounter someone who is sending out very different energies to yours, there will be a battle for supremacy between you on an energetic level. Which one of you is going to win? Take note of the physical impact this experience has on you. Can you feel tension in any one or more of your chakras?

## what happens to our auras when we are angry

When someone is angry, their aura becomes suffused with deep red. This is different from the bright red that indicates vitality and health. If the person is able to express his anger, perhaps by shouting at someone or kicking a door, red blobs of energy will shoot out of his aura at the same time. If he smothers his anger for some reason, it will be held within his aura unless he finds some way to release it. If he habitually holds on to his anger, it will eventually form an energy block within his aura and could lead to a chronic ailment or some form of debility.

*Red clouds in a person's aura can symbolize vibrant energy but they can also show anger and jealousy.*

# the cords between us

**When you establish a relationship with someone, your auras are linked by many cords. In a loving relationship, most of the cords will emanate from the heart chakras, but there will be cords connecting the other chakras as well. Because these cords are made of energy, they can stretch for thousands of kilometres if necessary, which is why friends are able to maintain strong emotional or intellectual connections even when they live on opposite sides of the world.**

## keeping cords healthy and positive

You might imagine that the cords in a happy relationship do not need any attention because they are so positive and loving. However, less favourable cords can also be created between two people, based on such emotions as neediness, jealousy, irritability or dependency. All these emotions are perfectly normal but sometimes they can prevent a relationship moving forward and growing.

It is therefore a good idea to check the cords between you and the people in your life every now and then, and to remove any cords that are difficult or unhelpful. Removing these cords will not stop you liking and loving each other; cord-cutting does not automatically lead to the severing of a relationship. However, if the relationship is already over, you may want to cut all the cords between you or leave only a few intact.

## cutting cords

1 Choose a time when you will not be disturbed and put yourself in a relaxed state (see page 31). Close your eyes. Choose the relationship you want to work on and picture the person concerned standing in front of you. Now picture yourself facing them. Mentally enclose each of your auras in its own protective bubble of light.

2 Observe the energetic connections between your two auras and look for the cords that connect you. If you cannot see these cords with your mind's eye, know that they are there and work with your intuition. What do these cords look like? Are they all healthy and pleasant, or do some look angry or challenging? For instance, you might see a chain connecting you, or what looks like a piece of barbed wire.

3 With an imaginary pair of scissors, cut through the middle of the first cord you want to sever. Pull your half of the cord out of your aura and place it to one side. Seal the place where the cord was attached to your body with golden light to stop the area leaking energy. Now do the same to the other person's half of the cord.

4 Continue this process with each cord that looks problematic, making sure that you seal the place where it was attached to your body with golden light. When you have finished, set light to the pile of cut cords. Watch them burn and know they are being transmuted into positive energy that will be absorbed by you and the other person.

5 Thank the other person for working with you on this exercise, then surround her aura with another protective bubble of white light. Watch her walk away. Now surround your own aura with a bubble of white light and take several deep breaths. Make sure you are fully grounded (see page 95) before standing up.

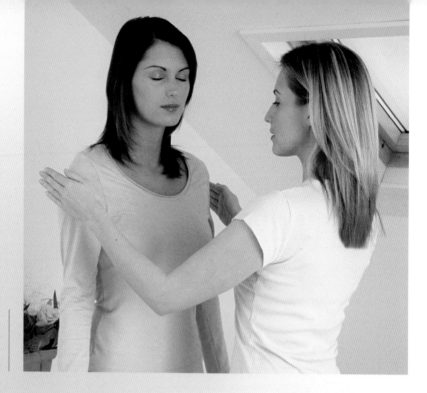

*One of the quickest pick-me-ups when you feel tired or emotionally exhausted is to have your aura brushed. You will immediately feel lighter, clearer and more positive.*

# auric influence

**Here are some exercises that build the auric connection between you and a friend or partner. These exercises will help you to tune into each other's auras while having fun, and they will also increase your ability to sense auras with your hands and your intuition.**

## finding the right partner

You need to work with someone who is at least ready to believe in the existence of auras, even if she has never seen or felt one before. These exercises will not work if you practise them with someone who is an out-and-out cynic and who wants the exercises to fail in order to prove her point. You must choose someone who is open-minded and receptive to new ideas, and who will not give up after a few minutes.

Ideally, you should keep practising with your chosen partner. As you become more adept at sensing one another's auras, you will be able to invent new ways of building the auric connection between you. Be creative and have fun.

## auric brushing for partners

1 This is an excellent exercise if one of you is tired at the end of a long day or has had a difficult experience. Put yourself into a relaxed state (see page 31). Ask your partner to stand in front of you, feet slightly apart and hands by her sides.

2 Place your hands about 15 cm (6 in) away from either side of your partner's head and sweep them downwards towards her neck. Shake off the energy you have accumulated on your hands into an imaginary receptacle. Now sweep down the front and back of your partner's head and shake off the energy.

3 Sweep down each part of your partner's body in turn. Do not forget to sweep down her arms and legs, and to sweep over her feet. When you have finished, ask for the discarded energy to be transformed into positive energy.

## pushing and pulling

1 Stand facing your partner with your feet slightly apart. You should both raise your hands so your palms are facing each other. Move your two hands towards your partner's hands, so they are close but not touching.

2 Hold your palms about 5 cm (2 in) away from each other for a couple of seconds. Can you feel anything, such as heat or cold? Now gradually move your palms apart and then towards each other again. Can you feel anything now?

3 Continue to move your palms backwards and forwards until you are aware of the space between your hands. It will start to feel bouncy and elastic, and as you and your partner move your hands apart you will both be able to feel the energy stretching. As you move your hands closer together, you will feel the energy compressing so there is a noticeable resistance between your two palms.

4 Keep playing with the energy between your hands, seeing how far you can move them apart and still be aware of it. If you keep practising, you may eventually end up on opposite sides of the room while still able to maintain a strong energetic connection.

# taking it one step further

**One of the best ways of developing your ability to sense auras is to work with another person. In this way, you can give each other feedback and work on any areas that you think need more practice. If possible, you should practise the exercises here with the same partner you have already been working with because you will be familiar with one another's energy.**

## building the connection

These exercises will help you to build and strengthen the auric connection between you and your partner. As you continue to work with each other, you will become more attuned to one another. You may even find that this spills over into the rest of your life, creating a beneficial effect when you are not practising on each other.

## circles of energy

1 Choose a time when you will not be disturbed, and when you are both relaxed. Build up the auric connection between you by practising the pushing and pulling exercise (see page 115) for a couple of minutes until you can feel the energy between you.

2 Now hold out your right arm and close your eyes, so you cannot see what is happening. The other person should stand about 30 cm (1 ft) away and draw squiggles and other shapes in the air over your right arm. How close does the second person have to be to your arm before you can sense the movement in your aura? Continue to practise this, with you receiving the sensations and the other person creating them; then swap over. Do not worry if you cannot feel the sensations very well at first. Keep practising until you can both describe the shapes that are being drawn in your auras.

# grandmother's footsteps

1 Once again, choose a time when you will not be disturbed and do not have to hurry. Ideally, you should work on a carpeted floor indoors or on a stretch of grass outside to muffle your footsteps. Attune your auras by practising the pushing and pulling exercise (see page 115) for a few minutes.

2 Stand with your back to your partner. Put your hands over your ears so you cannot hear what she is doing and close your eyes. If you are in a room, stand facing a wall so there is plenty of space behind you.

3 Stand still and concentrate on the sensations you are receiving in your aura. Your partner should stand about 3.5 m (12 ft) away and then slowly walk towards you. Keep monitoring the sensations in your aura until you can sense that your partner has just started to invade your aura. You will know this because of a tickling, prickling or shivering sensation down your back. Call out 'Stop!' and ask your partner to mark the point she has reached by placing a small object, such as a pencil, on the ground. Now repeat the exercise. Has the distance at which you can sense your partner changed? Swap roles so your partner can register the sensations in her aura.

# YOUR AURA AND EVERYDAY LIFE

Your aura is not something for special occasions or which only comes out at night. It is working with you and for you all day, every day. So it makes sense to work with it, thereby becoming more familiar with it and more practised at tuning into it.

If you listen to your aura, it will give you valuable information about a whole host of everyday activities, from the colour of the clothes you choose to put on when you get dressed to the foods that are good for you and the objects you allow into your home. You will discover which areas of your home are good places for relaxing and which have a more energetic atmosphere. These techniques are especially useful if you are having difficulty sleeping and want to find a better position for your bed. This chapter will also tell you how to use your aura when you are away from home and in unfamiliar surroundings. You will discover how to clear strange beds of the energy they have absorbed from their previous occupants and how to scan restaurant menus for dishes that you will enjoy. If you practise these techniques, you will find that your aura never lets you down.

# your aura at home

**Every inanimate object has its own aura. This means that every object in your home, from your hairbrush to your kitchen table, has an aura that you can discern with practice.**

## looking at the aura of favourite furniture

Take a few seconds to decide which is your favourite piece of furniture. What do you love about it? When you have some quiet time to yourself, try to sense and see its aura. Start by running the palms of your hands over its auric field, about 5 cm (2 in) away from its surface. Can you feel anything? Move your hand in and out of its auric field until you meet some energetic resistance, which will tell you that you are touching the outer edge of the furniture's aura. Is the aura the same depth throughout, or are some areas deeper than others?

*Your favourite chair will be doubly comfortable and enjoyable if you can place it in an area that feels relaxing and free of stress.*

## reading the auras of pets

Our pets have auras too. When your pet appears to be content for you to do so, you can observe its aura in exactly the same way that you would observe a fellow human's aura. Look for any energy blocks or other indications of problems. What colour is your pet's aura? Does this surprise you, or is it what you would have expected?

## creating a space to relax

In this exercise, you are looking for the best place in your home in which to relax. When you have found it, you could place a comfortable chair here, or even move your bed here if that is feasible. Work systematically through each room in turn.

1 In the first room, hold your hands out in front of you, palms facing outwards. Stand about 10 cm (4 in) away from the wall and scan it with your hands. Let your body register the emotions and energies you pick up. Do you feel excited, happy, anxious, ill? What does the area around the wall feel like? Is it hot? Does it feel busy or relaxed?

2 Keep working until you have scanned your entire home and have selected a suitable place. If you find an area with uncomfortable or unsettling energy, cleanse it with a singing bowl or by leaving a crystal there (see pages 86–88).

*The best way to cleanse second-hand objects is to wash them in warm, soapy water. If this will ruin them, you should mentally bathe them in white light or leave a bowl of sea salt near them for a few days.*

# choosing objects to buy

**Sometimes we are instinctively drawn to a particular object in a shop because we know we must have it. When this happens, there is an attraction between the object's aura and our own. On other occasions, however, we may dither between two objects, unsure about which one to buy.**

Some people are more indecisive than others, of course, and may struggle to make up their minds about almost everything. However, if you are normally decisive but you are faced with a display of identical objects and are suddenly unsure which one to buy, you can tune into the aura of each one. Hold your palm so it faces outwards and scan the aura of each item. Does one feel more inviting than the others? If you can see the auras, you will be able to choose the one that looks most attractive to you.

## second-hand objects

Once you begin to work with auras and understand their importance, you will never again bring a second-hand object into your home without scanning its aura first. Objects retain the energy of their owners, so that table you see in an antique shop will be impregnated with the energy of its previous owner and the energy of any important incidents that took place around the table. For instance, this might have been where the family ate their meals while laughing and enjoying one another's company, or it might have been where they ate in fraught silence, full of blistering resentment towards each other. All of this will have been absorbed by the table. The more sensitive you become to auras, the more you will be aware of this energy.

## mirrors

Be very choosy when acquiring a second-hand mirror. Mirrors absorb the energy of the people who use them and then reflect this energy back into the room. If you do not know who owned the mirror before you, you can cleanse the glass with salt water, provided this will not damage the frame of the mirror. If the frame is too fragile for this, leave a bowl of rock salt in front of the mirror for a week, changing it daily.

*Second-hand and antique mirrors can be very beautiful but they also need to be cleansed before use.*

## clearing other people's energy from objects

1 There are several ways to do this, depending on the object in question. Hot, soapy water will remove old energy from plates, cutlery, vases and similar objects. Second-hand clothes should always be washed or dry-cleaned before you wear them. It is not a good idea to buy second-hand shoes because, quite apart from the fact that they will have moulded themselves to fit someone else's foot shape, it will be difficult to remove that person's energy from them.

2 When you cannot wash the item in question, you can bathe it in white light. Ground yourself (see page 95), then imagine a beam of white light pouring down from the sky into your crown chakra and out through your heart chakra and the palms of your hands. Mentally direct all this light onto the object in question and know that all its stale energy is being removed.

# your aura while travelling

**Being away from home can be disorientating because you are being exposed to many new experiences and different energies. However, a few protective measures will help to keep you balanced and relaxed, especially if you will be spending the night in strange surroundings.**

## deciding where to stay

If you are planning your next holiday, you can dowse your prospective hotel in advance. If you see it in a brochure, simply hold your palm above the photograph of the hotel to test its aura. Does it feel welcoming or unfriendly? You can do the same thing if your hotel appears on a website. If you are wondering which country or area of a country to visit, dowse an atlas or road map with your palms or with a pendulum (see page 49). If you are looking for a hotel or guesthouse while on your travels, stand on the opposite side of the road and study its aura.

*Experiment by quickly scanning your food before you eat it. As you become more adept your hands and intuition will register increasing amounts of information.*

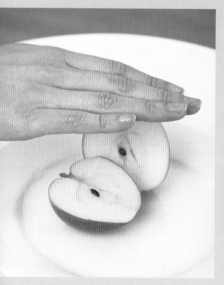

## deciding what to eat

Some people love eating unfamiliar food, while others feel unnerved by it. If you are unsure whether you will enjoy a particular dish on the menu, look at the words and ask your body how you will feel when you have eaten the food. Will you feel good? Will you feel slightly unwell? You can also look down the menu to see which entry looks brightest. Do not attempt to read the words; simply look for the most attractive part of the menu. Only then should you read the words, and usually you will find that you have picked an appetizing dish.

When you are served food or drink, you can test its aura by holding your palm a short distance above it. Pay attention to the sensations you get in the centre of your palm. Does it feel drawn to the food or drink or repelled by it? If your hand is repelled, you might enjoy the food or drink but it will not be very good for you.

## protecting your aura from fellow travellers

Travelling conditions are often very crowded and uncomfortable, especially on trains and planes. You can protect your aura by strengthening your auric shield (see page 107) and by frequently checking that you are grounded (see page 95). If you wish, you can also carry a piece of clear quartz next to your skin for added protection.

## cleansing the energy of a strange bed

1 We emit a lot of energy while we sleep. You should therefore cleanse a strange bed of energy before you get into it, to make it feel neutral and to enable you to relax enough to go to sleep quickly. Start by grounding yourself (see page 95). Stand on one side of the bed with your arms outstretched and your palms facing downwards.

2 Sweep your hands through the air above the bed, using long strokes. Deposit the swept energy in an imaginary container by your side (see page 79). Continue sweeping the bed until you have cleansed every bit of it. If you have a rose or clear quartz crystal with you, leave it in the centre of the bed to continue the purification process until you are ready to climb into bed.

# index

# acknowledgements

Executive Editor  Sandra Rigby
Editor  Kate Tuckett
Executive Art Editor  Sally Bond
Designer  Annika Skoog
        for Cobalt Id
Picture Library Manager
        Jennifer Veall
Production Manager  Louise Hall

**Corbis U.K. Limited** 92; /Lou Chardonnay 84; /Rick Gomez 77; /LWA/Stephen Welstead 104. **Fortean Picture Library** 17. **Getty Images**/Jasper James 66; /Victoria Pearson 50. **Octopus Publishing Group Limited** 52, 64; /Frazer Cunningham 7, 19, 20, 27, 29, 31, 33, 34, 41, 45, 46, 47 left, 47 right, 49, 53, 58, 60, 61, 65, 69 top, 72 top, 81 left, 81 right, 83 left, 83 right, 87, 95, 97 inset, 100, 101, 103, 106, 114, 115, 117, 122, 124, 125; /Janeanne Gilchrist 110; /Steve Gorton 121; /Andy Komorowski 99 top centre, 99 centre, 99 bottom right, 99 bottom centre right; /Gary Latham 2, 97; /David Loftus 67 top; /Mike Prior 5, 11, 13, 23, 24, 37, 48, 63 right, 67 bottom, 68 top, 69 bottom, 70 top, 71 bottom, 73 top, 73 bottom, 75, 88 top, 89, 91, 94, 111, 113; /Guy Ryecart 99 top right, 99 bottom centre, 99 top centre right; /Peter Pugh-Cook 18, 63 left, 85, 93; /William Reavell 120; /Russell Sadur 1, 8, 55, 56 left, 56 right, 68 bottom, 70 bottom, 71 top, 72 bottom, 79, 86, 96, 107, 109, 119. **Photolibrary Group**/Rebecca Emery 51; /Van Osaka 88 bottom; /Julie Toy 59, 105. **The Picture Desk/The Art Archive**/British Library 39; /Scrovegni Chapel, Padua/Dagli Orti 14. **Science Photo Library**/Michel Vard, Peter Arnold Inc. 16. **Skinner, Inc.** 123.